© 2015 Free - Winning the War Against Sexual Immorality by Jason John Cowart

For contact or more information, please visit www.abookcalledfree.com or www.jasonjohncowart.com.

ISBN-10: 1519434006
ISBN-13: 978-1519434005

All rights reserved. No part of this publication may be reproduced, stored in a retrieval system, or transmitted in any form or by any means, for example, electronic, photocopy, recording, etc., without the prior written permission of the author and/or publisher. The only exception is brief quotations in written for the purpose of reviews.

Unless otherwise indicated, excerpts from the Bible taken from:

Holy Bible, New Living Translation
Copyright © 1996, 2004, 2007 by Tyndale House Foundation.
Used by permission of Tyndale House Publishers Inc., Carol Stream, IL 60188. All rights reserved.

Translations also referenced:
New King James Version.
Copyright © 1982 by Thomas Nelson, Inc. Used by permission. All rights reserved.

The Holy Bible, English Standard Version (ESV)
Copyright © 2001 by Crossway, a publishing ministry of Good News Publishers. Used by permission. All rights reserved. ESV Text Edition: 2011

Library of Congress Cataloging-in-Publication Data
Cowart, Jason John 1979-
   Free : winning the war on sexual immorality : Jason John Cowart—1st ed.
    p. cm.
   1. Sex—Religious aspects—Christianity. 2. Temptation. 2. Christian men—Religious life.

Printed in the United States of America
2015

This book was written for those
who are slaves to sin.
No matter how you got there,
God wants to set you free.

"For freedom Christ has set us free"
Galatians 5:1
English Standard Version (ESV)

FREE

*Winning the War Against
Sexual Immorality*

Pastor Jason John Cowart

INDEX

INTRODUCTION	2
CHAPTER ONE The Problem	4
CHAPTER TWO Ground Rules	8
CHAPTER THREE The Spiritual Side	16
CHAPTER FOUR The Heart	30
CHAPTER FIVE The Required Tools	33
CHAPTER SIX The Practical Tools	48
CHAPTER SEVEN Questions	58
CHAPTER EIGHT Freedom	66
FINAL THOUGHTS The Aftermath	72

INTRODUCTION

This book was created for the purpose of freedom. Too many people, especially young teenage men, are completely enslaved to sexual immorality. I have had countless conversations with teenagers, even grown men and women, about the issue of sexual immorality. Typically, sexual immorality takes the form of pornography, but we are living in a world that is so super-charged sexually, and so many, even young teenagers, have already engaged in sexual relations. Sadly, I can only see it getting worse.

There are two parts of this book. One deals with the spiritual side of this issue and the other provides practical tools to help you overcome. I don't just believe in the information in this book because it is good advice. I have lived it. These tools helped me overcome sexual immorality in my own life.

As a person who has struggled with this sin, I can honestly say that I wish I had learned this information when I was a teenager. I have, unfortunately, failed sexually, and as a result suffered a great deal of heartache and pain because of my sins. I thought what I was doing was what I wanted. I thought it was just fun. I thought it would satisfy me. All of those were lies. They were lies that the world fed me. They were lies that the entertainment industry fed me. They were lies the enemy fed me. But, rather than focusing on God and living to please him, I took the bait, choosing sin that will never satisfy over purity and honoring God.

To think that sexual immorality satisfies, back then, seemed so real. Now, after going through the process, I see how desperately wrong I was. I see how it affected more than just me, but my future wife as well. "I was wrong" is the understatement of the century.

This book represents the information that I pass on to those with who I counsel, but it also represents the path I took to get free from this sin. The good news - no, the great news - is that not only did God set me free, he restored what I had allowed the enemy to destroy.

My hope, my prayer, is that this book finds people before they go through this battle. I pray they would read and apply the truths found within to their lives so they never have to go through it all.

However, if you are reading this and you have fallen into the sin of sexual immorality, I want you to know that you haven't gone so far that you are out of reach. Your life is not over. As long as you have breath, you have purpose, and I promise, if you will read this, apply the truths, and allow God to deliver you, the freedom you have only dreamed about, you'll have. You'll find that it is the freedom that God intended for you from the beginning. Take heart! You are on the road to receiving that freedom.

I am proud of you for taking this step. These steps worked for me, they have worked for so many others, and I trust they will work for you.

When God created you, he started something great. Whether you have already fallen, or are on the verge, I want you to take in this passage that carried me through this process. Let it do the same for you. Philippians 1:6 says,

> "And I am certain that God, who began the good work within you, will continue his work until it is finally finished on the day when Christ Jesus returns."

Stick to the process. God is not finished with you. He began something great in you, and no matter how bad you think it is, God will forgive you, he will restore you, and he will complete in you what he began.

Be blessed, friend.
Jason

CHAPTER 1

THE PROBLEM

When I was young, sixth or seventh grade, I was playing around outside, as I often did. During the late eighties and early nineties, parents weren't so worried about kids going outside. it was a different time, I suppose. We lived along a highway, and a large plot of land, dense with a pine forest, was on the other side. I would often go into the forest and play. It was a ton of fun for a young guy. Thinking back on it now, I kind of miss those days. Things were much simpler!

One day, I was going across the road into the woods and saw something laying on the ground. I walked over to it and discovered a magazine, loaded from cover to cover with naked women. Until that moment, I hadn't seen pornography before. It was an odd moment: I knew I shouldn't look at it, but curiosity got the better of me. I took it across the road and placed it in a spot in the forest. My trips into the forest changed from that day on, as I would go back and look at it often.

After years of fighting pornography addiction, during a time of prayer God reminded me of that moment. I have often wondered if the person who threw that magazine on the road was having a moment of clarity and decided, once and for all, to get rid of it. I wondered if their moment of freedom was my moment of shackling. That is just speculation, of course, but I can tell you for sure, that is when this war in my life began.

The problem is that, at that moment, without me really even comprehending what was going on, the devil created a stronghold in my life. I should have rejected what I saw, but, because I opened the door when sexual immorality and lust were knocking, it entered, and worse, it made a home in me. That one moment in my life started a chain reaction of events that placed me in the middle of a war for my purity, but so much more. I had a problem.

The problem with sexual immorality is not just that it is not pleasing to God, but what it brings with it. We can clearly see in 1 Thessalonians 4:3-5 that sexual immorality is not God's desire for us.

> "God's will is for you to be holy, so stay away from all sexual sin. Then each of you will control his own body and live in holiness and honor—not in lustful passion like the pagans who do not know God and his ways."

Looking towards the end of that verse, we see that not only is immorality not God's plan, a person who engages in sexual immorality is compared to someone who doesn't even know God.

When I stepped into a lifestyle of sexual immorality, I put myself on this course of sin and sorry's that brought a ton of issues to the table I had not dealt with before. I thought I was just looking at something I shouldn't look at and engaging in an activity that tends to follow viewing porn. But what I didn't realize at the time, simply because of my young mind, was that I was separating myself from God. I was driving a wedge in our relationship. I loved God, but this stronghold had taken root and I had fallen for the trap. It created a horrible dissonance between God and I.

After a while of dealing with this back and forth between sin and sorry, I began to realize the impact that this sin was really having on me. My relationship with God was strained. My view of women changed. Lust became a constant issue that I had to fight. Masturbation became a serious problem. I didn't realize what really came with this sexually immoral package, and as a result I suffered from the penalties that it brought with it.

But the impact didn't stop with me.

When sin takes a foothold, it brings friends. What began as a problem with porn and masturbation became a real issue when I started dating in high school. Now, I wasn't having sex on a daily basis, but I was not living a pure lifestyle either. And if we think about Jesus told us about adultery, that even the thought of it is sinful, then I might as well have been having sex with those I dated.

One thing anyone who has had this struggle understands is how this stronghold seems to grow. It may start with something soft-core, maybe not even pornography by the definition, but you are left unsatisfied after a while. It is this insatiable desire that never seems to be fulfilled, so you find yourself looking at harder and harder pornography, and that eventually turns into sexual acts with another person. Sexual immorality never stays the same. It always grows. It always wants more.

There have been a ton of celebrities who have had crazy sexual issues that have come out. Unfortunately, we have seen many pastors fall to sexual sins. I guarantee you the sins at the height of their downfall were not where they started. For so many, it was something seemingly insignificant that worked its way into their lives and just continued to grow. That is how it happened for me. A random photo paved the way for a decade of struggle.

Things got worse when I went to college. I pledged a fraternity, and while I can't even remember kissing a girl as a pledge/active, I was constantly surrounded by pornography. Between what I could see from magazines, and the fact that the internet was quickly becoming a place to find porn for free, I was in a mess. I was destroying myself. I couldn't see 1 Corinthians 6:18.

> "Run from sexual sin! No other sin so clearly affects the body as this one does. For sexual immorality is a sin against your own body."

I would have seasons of strength where I would be able to abstain for periods of time. It made me feel like I was overcoming it. But then I would fail again. If it wasn't looking at porn on the internet, it was always a girl. Every time God was about to do something huge in my life, a girl would come along. It was almost like the devil could guess what I would fall for. That was sarcasm.

Here is what is really insane about this story: God was still using me to do some amazing things in ministry. That was one of the parts that was the hardest. I was struggling so hard with sexual immorality, but I was having success in what I was doing ministerially. I know you may feed the urge to judge me here, thinking, "How could he be doing all of this but still doing ministry?" That is a fair question.

To be honest, I was scared to death to tell anyone. I was afraid of being looked down on. I was afraid that I would lose everything I had worked for. I was scared of God, even. I would make these deals with God that if he would just hold on for a little longer I would overcome it. The enemy had me gripped by fear and convinced that I could overcome this on my own. "I can fix this before anyone finds out." What an unbelievable lie. That lie had me bound for years, over a decade.

In the months before I met the woman who would be my wife, I began to experience some breakthrough. God showed me the depth of the devastation, but it wasn't until I proposed to my then girlfriend that I saw how bad it really was.

Even worse than what sexual immorality was doing to me inside, was what it would do to the person I would eventually marry.

When she learned about it all, the pornography, the sexual sins, she was heartbroken. And because she was, I was. The only thing worse that knowing your wife is heartbroken is knowing it was you were the one that made her that way. It was as if I had cheated on her, and to be honest, I had. Before I ever knew her name, I had given her reward away.

Friend, I am telling you all of this so that you can see just how devastating this sin is. Whether you are deep into pornography, or you are having sex outside of marriage, even if you are married and currently engaged in extramarital affairs, you need to know that you are bringing destruction into your life on a grand scale.

That is the problem. But God has a solution.

I want to be free. Say those words out loud. You are reading the story of a man who was once bound, but now I am free. It doesn't mean that I don't get attacked anymore. I'm sorry to say that isn't true. I do still sense the attack, especially working with youth because what attacks them attacks me. But I can say this now, and really mean it, "I am free." I am. I am free.

It isn't because I followed some steps and said some words. It is because I allowed God to destroy strongholds, change my heart, and renew my mind. I am free, and if you are willing to allow God to change your heart and go through the process of renewing your mind, you can be free too.
Man, what a problem. Man, what an enemy. But praise God, what a Savior! You are going to be set free. Focus on that. When you begin to doubt, remind yourself that it is going to happen. Activate your faith and remind yourself over and over,

"For freedom Christ has set us free" Galatians 5:1 (ESV)

Do you believe it? Believe it!

However, before we jump in, I think it is important to set some ground rules. Let's talk about those in the next section.

CHAPTER 2

GROUND RULES

Over the course of 15 plus years in worship, youth, and college ministry, I have talked with tons of teenagers about sexual purity, including sexual activities, sexual relations, and, predominately, pornography. It seems that this is a struggle that is all too common in our world today. A part of this is the fact that teenagers are raging with hormones, their bodies are changing, and the development of their sexuality is in full swing. But that is only a part of it. The other part is that we live in a severely sexualized environment in which we can't go a single day without having some form of a sexual encounter at some point, be that advertisements, scantily or tightly clothed people, etc. Perhaps you aren't engaged in overt sexual activity every day, but the culture itself is permeated with sexual content. Everywhere you go, anything you do, there is something sexual trying to influence you. Desi and Lucy didn't even sleep in the same bed, but now, soft-core pornography is commonplace on primetime television.

That being said, we have to get to a place in our lives where, though we are surrounded by it, sexual immorality has no influence. That is hard. It is hard to live in a kennel and not smell like a dog. True enough. But we can live in this world, as sick and evil as it may be, without indulging in the sin it peddles.

This is where most teenagers - everyone if we really think about it - find themselves when it comes to sexual immorality: a battle to live in the world but not do what the world does. No one is immune to the attack, but that doesn't mean we have to lose the battle. This book is designed to help you win the battle, and, ultimately, win the war over sexual immorality in your life.

Before we really dig in, though, we need to set some ground rules. There are some things you need to understand from the onset if you are going to beat sexual immorality.

1. The battle is always spiritual.
There are many out there who would say, "If drinking is a problem, then don't go to a bar." This is great advice, and before the last page of this

book, you will get practical advice just like that. But there is something else that applies here, and that is a spiritual side that has to be addressed. Ephesians 6:12 tells us,

> "For we are not fighting against flesh-and-blood enemies, but against evil rulers and authorities of the unseen world, against mighty powers in this dark world, and against evil spirits in the heavenly places."

Some of our battle is definitely physical, but we cannot negate the spiritual. Sexual immorality, lust, perversion, these are all spirits that have a single mission in mind, and that is your destruction. If we are going to deal with sexual immorality in our lives, then we are going to have to understand that the battle is not just flesh and blood. There is evil at work around us that is hell-bent - literally - on destroying us and the destiny that God has for us.

Some may have a hard time believing in supernatural things like evil spirits attacking. You need to believe it. Demonic forces are real and they are attacking you. They are constantly seeking that weak spot in order to break in and destroy. The Bible tells us that the angels around the throne are beyond counting (Rev. 5, Heb. 12). We are also told that a third of the heavenly host fell with Satan (Rev. 12). That is a lot of evil that has been up to something for all these years, and that something is enticing humanity to sin.

There is a spiritual battle going on here. The good news is that we have a spiritual response. 2 Corinthians 10:3-5 says,

> "We are human, but we don't wage war as humans do. We use God's mighty weapons, not worldly weapons, to knock down the strongholds of human reasoning and to destroy false arguments. We destroy every proud obstacle that keeps people from knowing God. We capture their rebellious thoughts and teach them to obey Christ."

This is great news! There is a spiritual battle, but God has made spiritual weapons available so we can win.

2. Some of it is physical

While the battle against sexual immorality is always spiritual, there are, as well, some areas of your life that are flesh and blood physical that you are going to have to address in order to overcome this issue of sexual immorality. Some things are going to have to change. Some habits are going to have to be broken. Some rules are going to have to be levied and followed. You are going to have to take some physical actions and make some actual decisions in order to overcome.

This book is going to show you a variety of techniques, actions, and preemptive steps that can help you avoid falling into the trap that the enemy is setting before you. You are going to get some very practical counsel that will help you recognize the attack and give you the opportunity to actually take the way of escape that God promises you. (1 Cor. 10:13).

3. Most importantly, you have to be saved and filled with the Holy Spirit for any of this to work.
Sometimes Kroger has a sale. Well, honestly I think they always have something on sale, but in order to get the benefit of the sale, I have to have a Kroger card, that little thing you put on your keychain with the barcode gives you access to the sale. Without it, I can't get the benefits.

The same goes with Jesus. If you don't have Jesus, then you can't get the benefits that come with that relationship. In fact, it goes even deeper than that. If you don't have a relationship with Jesus Christ, it means you are still enslaved to sin. It is your master. Before we can get free of sexual immorality, the Son has to set us free from slavery to sin, not just sexual sin.

Consider Romans 7:14-24 where Paul talks about the struggles in his life before he met Jesus:

> "So the trouble is not with the law, for it is spiritual and good. The trouble is with me, for I am all too human, a slave to sin. I don't really understand myself, for I want to do what is right, but I don't do it. Instead, I do what I hate. But if I know that what I am doing is wrong, this shows that I agree that the law is good. So I am not the one doing wrong; it is sin living in me that does it.
>
> And I know that nothing good lives in me, that is, in my sinful nature. I want to do what is right, but I can't. I want to do what is good, but I don't. I don't want to do what is wrong, but I do it anyway. But if I do what I don't want to do, I am not really the one doing wrong; it is sin living in me that does it.
>
> I have discovered this principle of life—that when I want to do what is right, I inevitably do what is wrong. I love God's law with all my heart. But there is another power within me that is at war with my mind. This power makes me a slave to the sin that is still within me. Oh, what a

miserable person I am! Who will free me from this life that is dominated by sin and death?"

Without Jesus, we are more than merely people who are sinful; we are slaves to sin. A slave has to obey his master or else. A slave has no choice. A slave has no ability to do anything but what the master says. Sin rules over us and lurks within us. Paul, in this passage, relates the agony of that reality. At the end, he begs, "Who will free me?" In Romans 7:25, we find out the answer.

> Without Jesus, we are more than merely people who are sinful; we are slaves to sin.

"Thank God! The answer is in Jesus Christ our Lord!"

Our salvation comes through Jesus Christ and him alone, not just for our souls, but from the tyranny of our former slave master, sin.

All of this is simply to reinforce the fact that if you don't have a relationship with Jesus Christ, then you can't be free from sexual immorality. If there is no Jesus, then there is no freedom from sin, period, across the board. It is simply impossible.

The second part of point number three is being filled with the Holy Spirit. We were just looking around Romans 7, but if you look a little further in Romans 8, you will find some very interesting things about the life Jesus has called us to live. We were never meant to live our lives under the strain of sin, and that includes sexual immorality. We have been called to the life of an overcomer, not just a conquerer but more than conquerers. Romans 8 is where we get those amazing verses that make us feel empowered! We are more than conquerors though Christ! But there is something we must see at the very beginning of this passage. Romans 8:1-2 says,

> "So now there is no condemnation for those who belong to Christ Jesus. And because you belong to him, the power of the life-giving Spirit has freed you from the power of sin that leads to death."

Because of our relationship with Jesus Christ, condemnation has gone. This is powerful because it frees us from the crushing guilt that comes with sin. Jesus convicts to show us our sin, but he never condemns us in our sin. The difference is that one builds you up while the other tears you down. But look at the last part of that verse: it is the Spirit of God that gives us the power over sin. This is why you need the Holy Spirit living within you. It is the very power of God to help you overcome, not just the attack, but the attack, the plan, the mission, the battle, the war, and the leader behind it all! And the Holy Spirit, this powerful conquering Spirit, is in you! That is almost unbelievable! It should reinforce in you how committed God is to seeing you set free, so committed to your freedom, in fact, that he is willing to live inside of you to give you the power to overcome! Amazing!

If Jesus Christ is not Lord of your life, and/or you know that you are not filled with the Holy Spirit, you need to address these things immediately. I'm not pressuring you, not forcing you, but we are talking about a God - the one true God - who literally gave everything for you. He's not trying to trick you or pull a fast one on you. He is simply offering a dead person a chance at life. The Bible tells us in Romans 10:9-10,

> "If you openly declare that Jesus is Lord and believe in your heart that God raised him from the dead, you will be saved. For it is by believing in your heart that you are made right with God, and it is by openly declaring your faith that you are saved."

Most translations say, "If you confess with your mouth." Over the course of this book you will find that confession is a huge part of deliverance. At this point, you need to be sure you have a relationship with Jesus. If you don't know whether Jesus is Lord or if you are filled with the Holy Spirit, odds are you aren't. If He is Lord and you are filled, you'll know it without a doubt.

Perhaps you know that you are not saved, but you want to be. This is easy! I would ask you to pray this prayer, out loud. There is nothing special about the prayer itself, but by confessing and believing, God honors your decision and saves your soul. Simply pray,

> "Dear God, I know I am a sinner. I was born into sin, I was a dead person with no hope of life. However, because of your love for me, even while I was a sinner, you died for me. I believe you died for my sins. You took my place. You paid my debt to make me right with you. I believe in you. I believe that you died and rose again on the third day. I confess you, Jesus Christ, as Lord. You are the way, the truth, and the life, and I receive the gift of salvation you offer if I believe in my heart that you died and rose again, and if I confess you as Lord, which I now do. Thank you for saving me Jesus. I am yours. Amen."

If you prayed that and meant it, welcome to the family! God promised Romans 10:9-10 to us, and if you meant it, he does too. You are a brand new creation now (2 Cor 5:17). What you were is gone. That means your sins, your past, your fears, your screw ups, your failures. Gone. And on top of that, Heaven is rejoicing! If you prayed to receive Jesus, please tell someone. Call a friend, find a pastor, find me on social media. Let it be known whose you are now.

The next step is being filled with the Holy Spirit. There are so many weird, fanatical ideas about what the Holy Spirit does in a person's life. You can find everything from snake-handling to rolling on the floor and every craziness in between. But let me just tell you, all of that is not what the Holy Spirit is about. In John 14, Jesus himself explains what the Holy Spirit is.

> Verses 16-17. "I will ask the Father, and he will give you another Advocate, who will never leave you. He is the Holy Spirit, who leads into all truth. The world cannot receive him, because it isn't looking for him and doesn't recognize him. But you know him, because he lives with you now and later will be in you."

> Verse 26. "But when the Father sends the Advocate as my representative—that is, the Holy Spirit—he will teach you everything and will remind you of everything I have told you."

The Holy Spirit is the third part of God (God is one God, but a Trinity of Father, Son, and Holy Spirit. See Matt 28:19) and is a helper given to us as a gift by God the Father to empower us to live the life God calls us to. The Holy Spirit produces fruit in our lives (Gal. 5:22-23), counter to the works of the flesh (Gal. 5:19-21). Jesus himself teaches that we need the Holy Spirit in order to fulfill God's purpose in our lives.

Just so we are on the same page when it comes to the infilling of the Holy Spirit, I believe there are two specific interactions we have with the Holy Spirit. The first is at salvation. The Bible tells us in John 6:44,

> "For no one can come to me unless the Father who sent me draws them to me, and at the last day I will raise them up." (Note* While the text says the Father draws, God the Father uses the Holy Spirit to accomplish this, as the Holy Spirit does what the Father asks and guides the one being drawn into truth, which is Jesus. See John 16:13).

This is the first interaction the Holy Spirit has with the soon-to-be convert, and this first interaction leads the convert to salvation.

Sadly, this is where many Christians stop. They have only been taught salvation from sin so you can go to Heaven. However, Jesus himself, in John 16 as mentioned before, made it abundantly clear that, once Jesus ascended, God the Father would give the Holy Spirit as an advocate, a helper. This is the second infilling, which is not about salvation, but about power. This power encounter gives the Christian what is necessary to actually live out the overcoming life found in Romans 8. Even Jesus was baptized and then had an experience where the Holy Spirit descended and settled upon him "like a dove" (Matt. 3:16).

All of this emphasizes how monumentally important it is to be filled with the Holy Spirit. This power encounter is necessary in order to overcome the works of the enemy in your life. Perhaps you have made Jesus Lord of your life, but you have not been filled with the Holy Spirit. If that is the case, just like receiving salvation, you can receive the Holy Spirit. There is no magic formula or special prayer to pray that "makes it happen." Just as you confessed Jesus as Lord and received the gift of salvation he offers, you can receive the Holy Spirit. Simply pray this prayer out loud and allow the Holy Spirit to fill you.

> "Father, I thank you for the precious gift of salvation that you have given to me through Jesus Christ. It is my desire to receive all that you have for me. It is your will that I be filled with the Holy Spirit, so I confess my desire to be filled now. I receive the gift of the Holy Spirit and pray that the Holy Spirit would fill me. I praise you God and thank you for filling me with the Holy Spirit. Holy Spirit, I pray you would lead me, guide me, empower me, and teach me in all things."

Now begin to praise God and thank him for saving you and filling you with the Holy Spirit. You may begin to feel this intensity in your body, this desire to speak praises to God. If you do, let it flow out. It may seem like a river of living water is about to rush out of you. That is the Holy Spirit moving in you. Just praise God. Allow him to take over. You may begin to speak syllables you've never heard, or a language that seems foreign to you. That is normal. What is happening is found in Romans 8:26.

> "And the Holy Spirit helps us in our weakness. For example, we don't know what God wants us to pray for. But the Holy Spirit prays for us with groanings that cannot be expressed in words."

If you experience this, don't be alarmed! Just continue to praise God for filling you with the Holy Spirit. Perhaps you don't feel like anything happened. Remember, this is a gift that is to be received, not something that has to be worked up. Pray to receive the Holy Spirit until you feel you have received him. Otherwise, please contact someone who can lead you through this process. It is important.

These two things, salvation and the infilling of the Holy Spirit, are the two best decisions you will ever make. If you prayed these prayers and meant it, your eternity is forever changed. If you prayed and sincerely meant those prayers, you are now a child of God, filled with the Holy Spirit, ready to get delivered from a sin that beforehand, you could never overcome! Praise God!

Now that we have some ground rules established, let's go through this process of setting you free. Understand some things here:

1. This is going to require some things of you.
2. Some things about your life are going to have to change.
3. You are going to have to confess some sin and ask for forgiveness.
4. You are going to have to repent, which means to turn away and walk away from sin.
5. You are going to have to be committed to doing what this book asks you.
6. You are going to have to include people in your life to help you with this struggle.
7. You need to understand that some parts are going to be easy, but others, very tough.

If you are willing to see this through, you are going to experience freedom from this life of immorality and you are going to experience a life that is peaceful, free, happy, and best of all, pure. You can do this. No more guilt-ridden sorries. No more last time promises. Freedom is waiting!

CHAPTER 3

THE SPIRITUAL SIDE

We've established in Ephesians 6 that there is a spiritual side this this issue of immorality. I don't want that to frighten you. I don't want you to think you are fighting a weirdo ghost that makes you look at naked people. While there is a spiritual enemy that wants you destroyed, there is a spiritual Advocate that is dedicated to seeing you succeed as well. Up until this point, you have listened to and obeyed the wrong side. After you learn what you are about to learn, you will see that not only is victory a possibility, it is your inheritance as a child of God!

Where Satan Rules
There are strongholds in our lives that we have to deal with in order to live the life God has called us to live. But to understand the strongholds, we need to understand that Satan has a dominion that we need to recognize. Ephesians 2:1-3 says,

> "Once you were dead because of your disobedience and your many sins. You used to live in sin, just like the rest of the world, obeying the devil—the commander of the powers in the unseen world. He is the spirit at work in the hearts of those who refuse to obey God. All of us used to live that way, following the passionate desires and inclinations of our sinful nature. By our very nature we were subject to God's anger, just like everyone else."

In 2 Corinthians 4:4. Paul tells us,

> "Satan, who is the god of this world, has blinded the minds of those who don't believe. They are unable to see the glorious light of the Good News."

In Acts 26:17-18, Jesus appears to then Saul, soon to be Paul, and tells him,

> "Yes, I am sending you to the Gentiles to open their eyes, so they may turn from darkness to light and from the power of Satan to God."

These verses, among several others, equates (spiritual) darkness to Satan and his domain, and light to God's. 1 John 1:5 tells us,

> "This is the message we heard from Jesus and now declare to you: God is light, and there is no darkness in him at all."

All of this is mentioned to illustrate that Satan rules darkness and is rightfully, if you will, present there.

Why is this important? Where there is darkness, Satan has dominion. And if Satan and the demonic host rules darkness, and you have darkness lurking within you, he rules there too. It is pretty hard to evict a king from his kingdom, and one of the reasons you may have struggled up to this point with failure in this area is because you have addressed the physical, but you have never dealt with the spiritual side, the darkness, the satanic strongholds, lurking within you.

> **Where there is darkness, Satan has dominion.**

The good news is that God is all about setting you free. God has never lost a fight with the enemy, and he won't start losing now. If you are struggling with sexual immorality, you have some darkness lurking within you. Begin asking the Holy Spirit to reveal those areas where Satan has dominion in your heart. As he does, write them down so that once you've read this book, you can deal with them. I'll leave you some space to do just that.

Look at the list that you just made. These are the strongholds that are bent on keeping you bound in a lifestyle of sexual immorality. You need to get free - you HAVE to get free - of these strongholds. They are going to destroy you eventually. It is time to get set free. Maybe you don't want to wait until the end of the book to break these strongholds. If you want to be free now, pray these words out loud and believe that God is setting you free.

> "Father, I confess (read each one you wrote down) as sin. I have allowed darkness into my life by my own choices. I confess that as sin. By the Holy Spirit, I pull down every stronghold that the enemy has built in my life, whether it is by my own sin or ignorance, whether I know the stronghold by name or not, in the name of Jesus. In Jesus' name, I rebuke strongholds the enemy has leveraged against me, and I rebuke every unclean spirit that is influencing me, including the spirits of lust, sexual immorality, fornication, perversion, homosexuality, (name any other stronghold that you wrote down) and command them to leave, as it is written in James 4:7 that if I submit to God and resist the devil, he will flee. I thank you God that you desire purity for me, and I choose purity now. I ask your light to shine in the places that were dark in me. Fill those places with your Holy Spirit, Father. I renounce every stronghold of the enemy in my life and thank you for setting me free by the power of the Blood of Jesus and by the Holy Spirit. In Jesus' name I pray these things, Amen."

They are words on a page, but if you prayed that and meant it, then you have just experienced a major step to being set free. They say the first step is realizing you have a problem. Fair enough, but by confessing these strongholds have ruled over you, and by asking God by the power of the Holy Spirit to destroy them, you just initiated this process of complete and total freedom in your life.

Now that you understand that Satan has a dominion and that it is darkness in which he dwells, and that you have addressed that darkness, let's talk about how the enemy attacks so you can learn to spot his traps. You are free, so let's talk about some ways you can stay that way.

Understanding The Attack
In order to defeat the enemy, it helps to understand his attack. The enemy rarely, if ever, comes at you with a full frontal assault, bringing everything he has. This is like the Braveheart, charging the field, everyone to the fight, type of attack. If you look over the entire Bible, the only time he attacks like that is in the book of Revelation when he fights the final battle. The attack of the enemy ALWAYS starts with an single, simple

compromise, so simple and insignificant that you may have not even noticed it. Let me give you some examples.

Adam and Eve
The serpent didn't directly refute God at all. He simply implied that God might not have been 100% honest with them. He never said. "God is a liar." He only insinuated that God was hiding something from them. His plan was to cause man to fall, but the serpent didn't go with that angle. He just tempted them with something that seemed so small to derail them from their purpose.

David
When David committed adultery, he didn't wake up that day and say, "I think I'll be an adulterer today!" He simply walked out on his porch and happened to look across at the other house to see Bathsheba bathing on the roof. In that moment, he could have turned around and walked into his own house, called for his own wife, and you know what next. But the enemy came to him like he does to us and tempted him. "I wonder what it would be like to sleep with her." "Of course you have a wife, but she doesn't look like that." Then David took the bait and began to scheme, falling into one trap after the other, traps that led from lust to adultery to murder.

Jesus
Even with Jesus in Matthew 4 when he was tempted by Satan himself, Satan never came right at Jesus trying to force him to abandon God. He tried appealing to lust of the eyes, lust of the flesh, and the pride of life (1 John 2:16). The devil never told Jesus, "You are not the Son of God. You are a liar." He just slyly tempted him with fame and glory and riches.

The attack of the enemy is always off point, sneaky, and seemingly insignificant. Satan is the master of the sneak attack. You never trip over the boulder, only the pebble in the floor. The same happens with the devil. You'll rarely stumble from a major frontal attack, but you can barely resist the sneaky ploys that you least expect.

Since you understand this now, can you think of areas in your life where he has snuck in? Do you recognize moments where you've fallen for his hidden traps?

Maybe you are laying in your bed surfing the Internet at night when a random photo pops up of a woman with hardly anything on. It is in this moment that the enemy launches his attack.

"Wow, she's hot. I bet she has other photos like that if you click on her profile."

This is a spiritual attack. The moment you give in, the spirits of lust and impurity engage to lure you deeper into the fight. Perhaps you struggle with other sexual spirits like homosexuality, and that leads to diving into other photos that fuel the fire that has begun to rage inside of you. This is just a simple illustration, but it happens so often.

Maybe you have been proactive about what you look at online. If so, great! But what if you are at school or at work and a girl just happens to have on a shirt that shows every single curve? It is low-cut and shows more than you really need to see. It is at that very moment that Satan's dogs of war are let slip and you find yourself in a very real battle.

This is what I mean by a spiritual war that rages. It isn't Casper fighting the meanie-faced ghosts of the haunted house. It is the spirits who have aligned themselves with Satan raging war against God and his heavenly host, and you are caught in the middle. The war is for your soul! You have got to see that there is a fight that you are going to have to recognize and learn to win. The enemy we fight is real and he is actively seeking a weak spot in your wall.

You've heard it said before that Satan needs an open door. That is a lie. He just needs a cracked one. That is how he gets in. If you give him a cracked door, you've pretty well lost the battle. We can't give him a foothold. James 4:4 says,

> "Don't you realize that friendship with the world makes you an enemy of God? I say it again: If you want to be a friend of the world, you make yourself an enemy of God."

The reason this passage is true is because any flirtation with what the world offers provides the enemy with a sliver of darkness where he can plant his foot. In that moment, that sliver of darkness becomes the domain of the devil and is aligned against God. You may want to be cool with a certain group of friends or to have a specific person like you, but you cannot afford to befriend the darkness in this world even for a second. Otherwise, you've created a space for the enemy to set up his next siege tower.

So Now What

Now that you know how he attacks, you can make a battle plan. I want you to understand something up front that is going to make a huge difference in this fight: the enemy is never going to stop attacking you, especially on this matter of sexual immorality. I know that seems like a downer, but the truth is the truth. And if you have had a problem in this area, he definitely won't stop. He has found your weakness.

In the old days of war, the enemy would look for the weak spot in the castle wall. That is where they focused their attack. They knew if they could break down the wall, then they could enter the city. Once they got into the city, the battle was over. The enemy knows you very well. He knows where you are and what you do. He knows your schedule and your routine. He knows your weaknesses as well. If he knows all these things, it is simple to see that he is going to focus his attack there. It is simple logic.

2 Corinthians 10:3-5 says,

> "We are human, but we don't wage war as humans do. We use God's mighty weapons, not worldly weapons, to knock down the strongholds of human reasoning and to destroy false arguments. We destroy every proud obstacle that keeps people from knowing God. We capture their rebellious thoughts and teach them to obey Christ."

The battle is spiritual and we need to fight it spiritually. How? We have to pull down those strongholds. Easier said than done, huh? Well, on a no Jesus, no Holy Spirit level, yes. Impossible. But remember that you are saved by the blood of the Lamb. You are an overcomer by that blood and by your testimony. You now have, living inside of you, the very Spirit that raised Jesus Christ from the dead. If you try to take down the stronghold alone, you are going to fail, and miserably at that. But if you get Jesus and the Holy Spirit in the battle, it is game over for the stronghold.

One of the reasons that people have a struggle overcoming this issue in the past is simply because, for most, they try to do it in their own power. "Ok, here I go, cold turkey. I'm not going to look at porn anymore." You may get a week or two into it, maybe longer, but at some point, the wall will reveal its weakness and you will fail. Then you go through the "sorry" ritual where you ask God to forgive you one more time and that you'll never do it again, only to disappoint a month later. You simply cannot do this on your own in your own power.

What you will find is that if you step out of the way for a moment and allow the Holy Spirit to do what he does best, you will see this issue of pulling down these strongholds is not as hard as you thought. The Holy Spirit makes you free and liberates you from the law of sin that leads to death, not you. And when you allow the Holy Spirit to step in and fight, you'll see the battle sway God's way in seconds.

When I was struggling with sexual immorality, God gave me a vision that really helped me understand the role of the Holy Spirit in this battle. I was standing next to a massive siege tower that was positioned against the wall of a castle. I knew the castle represented my life and the siege tower was the work of the enemy, built up through spirits such as lust, sexual immorality, etc. In my hands was a rope attached to the tower. I was trying with all my might to pull it down. At times, it would seem like I was making progress. Other times, I'd be yanked around like a rag doll. I never could pull down the stronghold, no matter how hard I tried.

As the environment around me became clearer, I realized that I was trying to pull a single siege tower down, however, the enemy had several others stationed around the castle. They were all trying to get into the castle. I realized that even if I knocked down the siege tower of lust, another called pornography and another called sexual immorality were waiting.

At some point, I looked far off behind me, and I saw a man clothed brilliantly with shining armor seated upon a charger. A vast army stood behind him at the ready. In my vision, I knew the man was the Holy Spirit. Though the battle was raging around me, I knew he had been watching for a while. It was then that I saw the Holy Spirit mouth the words, "That is my job." In an instant, I knew why I could never defeat this enemy in my life. I was trying to fight a spiritual battle with a physical response. I thought I could have enough willpower to topple the stronghold, but in truth, I was never going to be able to overcome it, and not even budge it.

> I had to decide to allow the Holy Spirit to lead me into a new way to fight.

I had to decide to allow the Holy Spirit to lead me into a new way to fight, one where he was in charge and I listened and obeyed. The Holy Spirit has the power to do what I could never have done. I dropped the rope and instantly, the Holy Spirit and his army charged into the fray, and in a moment, the strongholds - all of them - were toppled, and the battle was over. The war continued, and I still had some steps to take, but for the first time, by the power of the Holy Spirit, I had won the battle.

It is amazing what can happen if we actually allow the Holy Spirit to do what he can do. This is not to say that just by being filled with the Holy Spirit, the battle is over. No, not at all. But by being filled with the Holy Spirit, you actually have the power to overcome the attack, power that you never had before.

This vision was revolutionary for me. It finally gave me the understanding as to why I was struggling so badly. Perhaps the same is true for you as well. So let's talk about some ways to wage war against the enemy. That vision God showed me was refreshing and really helped me focus on allowing the Holy Spirit to fight for me, but there were some spiritual responses that I had to do in order to overcome.

Renewing Your Mind
2 Corinthians 10:3-5 says,

> "For though we walk in the flesh, we do not war according to the flesh. For the weapons of our warfare *are* not carnal but mighty in God for pulling down strongholds, casting down arguments and every high thing that exalts itself against the knowledge of God, bringing every thought into captivity to the obedience of Christ, (NKJV)"

- We walk in flesh but don't war according to flesh. Got it.
- Our weapons are not carnal but mighty in God to pull down strongholds. Got it.
- We cast down every argument (or excuse) that exalts itself above God. Got it.
- Bringing every thought captive to the obedience of Christ. Let's chat about that one.

Your thought life is the most important piece in this puzzle, second to the presence of the Holy Spirit. The mind is an amazing thing that has unlimited potential, but it is also a potential playground for the enemy and his most favorite battleground. There is a mighty war that rages between your two ears and you needn't think for a moment it is not spiritual. If you can get this mind thing down, you will be well on your way. Let me explain.

The devil, like any human, cannot read your mind. He is not omniscient (all-knowing) like God is (see 1 Cor 2:6-8). Because he doesn't know everything, he cannot know what you are thinking. However, while he can't know what you are thinking, he can guess. How? History and responses to stimuli. Tell you what, pick a number 1-4. You picked three right? Another one: pick a number from 1-100. The first digit has to be even and the second digit second and first have to be different. You picked 67, right? Some of you did, some may not, but the vast majority of people will pick those numbers. It boils down to best chances based on observed behavior. Psychologists often use these illustrations to show how very predictable people really are.

Satan works just like this. If he knows you have a weak spot when it comes to looking at porn, he is going to tempt you with a photo. He doesn't know if it works or not until you act on it. The moment you act on it, he yells, 'CHARGE!" in the spiritual realm, and the battle begins. For many of us, with the first move, the battle is over.

This is why the mind is such a key part of the equation. What do you think "taking every thought captive" means? What does taking a captive look like in war? When you take a captive in war, you disarm them, you bind them, you render them no longer a threat. So what does that look like in terms of spiritually taking captive a thought?

First, you have to disarm it. Soldiers disarm a captive with a weapon of their own. So we have to figure out what weapons we have. If we look in Ephesians 6, we find the passage describing the armor of God. Helmet of salvation, breastplate of righteousness, loins gird about with truth, feet shod with the preparation of the Gospel of peace, the sword of the Spirit, which is the Word of God, and the shield of faith to quench the fiery darts of the enemy. Of that list there is only one weapon: the sword. The rest are defensive. You disarm a thought with the Word of God. When you speak the Word of God into your situation, that Word has the power to disarm the attack of the enemy. "I am bought with the Blood of Jesus Christ and I confess his promises over me that I am set free by the power of the Holy Spirit.!" You disarm it.

Second, you bind it. In Matthew 16, we see Jesus tell Peter after his confession of who Jesus is, that he will receive the keys to the Kingdom and whatever he binds on earth will be bound in heaven, and whatever is loosed on earth will be loosed in heaven. By the power of the Holy Spirit, you have the authority to bind the thought. I think it is very interesting that this phrase was the response immediately following Peter's declaration of who Jesus really was, in light of the fact that every thought must be made captive to the knowledge of God and the obedience of Christ. "I bind the works of the enemy in my life right now and command the enemy to flee in the name of Jesus."

Once you disarm and bind, the thought is no longer a threat. This whole dance is not something that is done in the physical realm, but in the spiritual.

Consider Romans 12:2.

> "Don't copy the behavior and customs of this world, but let God transform you into a new person by changing the way you think. Then you will learn to know God's will for you, which is good and pleasing and perfect."

Remember, winning the battle in your mind is a huge part of this war. Perhaps you have heard this phrase, but don't really know how to do that. Renewing your mind sounds complex, but it is really simple. Robert Morris, Senior Pastor of Gateway Church in Southlake, Texas said in *The Blessed Life*, "Mind renewal brings transformation." If you genuinely want to be transformed, you need to renew your mind and do it daily. Here's how:

1. Be consistent in Prayer
2. Get in the Word
3. Monitor your inputs

I once heard Pastor Robert teaching on renewing the mind and he said that each morning before his feet hit the floor, he prayed God would renew his mind. This is a guy who is the pastor of what I would call the healthiest church in America. This phenomenal pastor, still on a daily basis, prays God renew his mind by the Holy Spirit. It isn't complex. It is very simple.

> "Father, thank you so much for this day. I want to honor you today. I want to live a life that pleases you and brings you joy. I am asking you, by your Holy Spirit, to help me today. Help me renew my mind. Allow my thoughts to be about you and your Kingdom. Give me the tools I need to overcome any idle thought, any thought that would lead me into darkness. Purify my mind, Holy Spirit. Let me be led by you today. I thank you for your faithfulness God. Thank you for renewing my mind. In Jesus' name. Amen"

Praying a prayer like that does wonders. If you mean it, God means it. It isn't rocket science. It is simply you humbling yourself, submitting to God, and allowing the Holy Spirit to refresh your mind. This is in addition to your normal prayer time. God tells us that renewal of the mind is something we do, but you need to daily ask God to help you in that task.

On top of that, you have to get the Word in you. Psalm 119:11 says,

> "I have hidden your word in my heart, that I might not sin against you."

One of the keys to not sinning against God is to get his Word in you. Hide it deep within you. When you hide the Word of God in you, it is what comes out when the heat is on. Not only that, by hiding the Word within you, you learn powerful verses that will help you win in the moment the battle begins with temptation.

You Can Do This
Romans 8:1-2 says,

> "So now there is no condemnation for those who belong to Christ Jesus. And because you belong to him, the power of the life-giving Spirit has freed you from the power of sin that leads to death."

See the contrast of power that gives life and power that brings death. If you struggle with sexual temptations, you have to understand that the spiritual battle is being waged and you have a choice. You can either lose miserably, fighting to the death, and never overcoming, or you can do what God wants by allowing the Holy Spirit to fight your battle, letting him guide you, renewing your mind, and allowing God to lead you to victory. You need to realize that there are serious spiritual strongholds, serious spirits, that are determined to destroy you. This fight is spiritual! You need to respond spiritually!

Christian, you have, within you, the power that raised Jesus Christ from the dead! If you will use the tools God has given us to overcome these spirits, to pull down the strongholds, to take captive every lustful, perverse thought, you will not only conquer, you will more than conquer!

God has a beautiful destiny for you, and no matter how far down this rabbit hole of sexual immorality you have gone, you are never too far where he can't reach you. Psalm 139 tells us,

> "I can never escape from your Spirit! I can never get away from your presence! If I go up to heaven, you are there; if I go down to the grave, you are there. If I ride the wings of the morning, if I dwell by the farthest oceans, even there your hand will guide me, and your strength will support me. I could ask the darkness to hide me and the

light around me to become night—but even in darkness I cannot hide from you. To you the night shines as bright as day. Darkness and light are the same to you."

You're never too far gone. You're never out of reach! But now that you know the spiritual war that goes on for your soul, and because of Jesus Christ and the Holy Spirit, you have the tools you need to destroy strongholds, rebuke spirits, and shine the light of Christ into the darkest parts of your heart. This should get you excited!

Staying Free
As we have addressed, if you are going to overcome sexual immorality in your life, you have to deal with the spiritual side. In my personal battle with this over the years, there were many times when I would be able to stay away for a period of time, but I would always find that I would fall again. It was a deadly cycle of promises, failures, and half-hearted apologies to God.

"God I promise that was the last time." I said that countless times. It was horrible, because I knew I was letting God down, I was compromising my commitment to him, I was worried that I was ruining my chances to serve him, and it was literally torture, because, just like Paul said in Romans 7, I wanted to do what was right, but there was this sin lurking within me. But I finally realized that I was trying to do something in the flesh that I could not defeat.

In Matthew 12, Jesus tells the religious leaders a simple phrase: "A kingdom divided against itself cannot stand." I was a person trying to use the flesh to respond to a spiritual battle. My flesh is not godly. My flesh is not good. Do a simple verse search on the flesh and you will find out some very unflattering things about it. (All verses from the ESV).

> Romans 8:8
> "Those who are in the flesh cannot please God."
>
> Galatians 5:16
> "But I say, walk by the Spirit, and you will not gratify the desires of the flesh."
>
> Romans 8:6
> "For to set the mind on the flesh is death, but to set the mind on the Spirit is life and peace."

Galatians 5:19-21

"Now the works of the flesh are evident: sexual immorality, impurity, sensuality, idolatry, sorcery, enmity, strife, jealousy, fits of anger, rivalries, dissensions, divisions, envy, drunkenness, orgies, and things like these. I warn you, as I warned you before, that those who do such things will not inherit the kingdom of God."

The flesh was doing nothing for me but leading me to death, to sin, to everything and more that you see in Galatians 5. I mean, look at the very first work of the flesh listed in verse 19: sexual immorality. How deceived I was! Try and try as I did, I was never able to overcome sexual immorality using the flesh, like I was trying to. I had the accountability partners. People had my passwords. I made those promises not to look anymore. It was all 100% flesh and it all 100% failed.

A kingdom divided against itself cannot stand. I could not overcome sin with flesh, with physical responses. I had to address the spiritual issue with a spiritual response.

That is what we just walked through. It is important that you address the strongholds in your life that keep you bent towards that sin. Just like people who have alcoholism in their family have natural tendencies towards alcoholism, I had a natural bent towards sexual immorality because of the strongholds I had allowed.

> Please don't believe the lie that just because a stronghold fell, the war is over.

But just as important as dealing with the spiritual side of getting free is understanding how you stay free.

In Matthew 12:43-45, Jesus tells how demons respond to being cast out. I bring this up because there are some very important truths we need to understand about this process.

"When an evil spirit leaves a person, it goes into the desert, seeking rest but finding none. Then it says, 'I will return to the person I came from.' So it returns and finds its former home empty, swept, and in order. Then the spirit finds seven other spirits more evil than itself, and they all enter the person and live there. And so that person is worse off than before."

Jesus clearly tells us what happens in this scenario. Once you are set free, the enemy leaves, but you need to understand very clearly that he will come back. Hear that again - the enemy will come back and attack you. In fact, Jesus told his audience that if they didn't take some steps afterward, the enemy would come back with seven more demons to help. Please don't believe the lie that just because a stronghold fell, the war is over. The enemy is not going to quit after a single battle is lost.

But Jesus said that while the enemy comes back, he is looking for something very specific: he looks to see if his room is still available.

Before, we talked about the darkness that lurks within our hearts. This is where the enemy dwells. It is like a room all carved out just for him. When Jesus says, "So it returns and finds its former home empty, swept, and in order," what he is telling us is that if there is not something that occupies that space left when the enemy left, he will return to it, and worse, bring seven roommates.

The point is that you have to deal with the stronghold, but follow up with the right steps in order to insure that the enemy doesn't have a place to come back to. The war is still raging. The good news is that we can actual win now because of the work of the Holy Spirit in our lives, but there are some specific steps that we have to take in order to stay free. Some of these are spiritual things, some of them are natural, physical things, but they are all intended to make sure that when the enemy returns to his old homestead, he finds that the Holy Spirit has taken up residence and there are no vacancies for him.

With that, let's spend some time talking about your heart and some practical steps you can take to make sure that you get free and stay free. Galatians 5:1 tells us,

> "So Christ has truly set us free. Now make sure that you stay free, and don't get tied up again in slavery to the law."

These tools are going to help make sure you don't go back to the former lifestyle you had before. Some of these steps are suggestions, some of them are things are required in order to stay free. Purpose in your heart right now that you will do the things that are required, and that you will explore the suggestions to see which tool is right for you.

My guarantee is this: if you will follow through with these practicals, use them when you are tempted, and determine that you are going to do what God asks no matter what, you will succeed.

CHAPTER 4
THE HEART

If you're an alcoholic, you shouldn't go to a bar. This is great advice. I think people should follow this advice. However, while it may be good advice, it is incomplete because the bar isn't the only place where alcohol is served. So "don't go to a bar" is only a piece of the puzzle. You've got to figure out ways to avoid booze when you aren't in a bar.

The same principle goes with sexual immorality.

"Don't go watch sexual movies." Great advice. You need to look on imdb.com for every movie you want to watch to make sure it doesn't have anything you shouldn't see in it. But what about those Victoria's Secret posters that are literally 10 feet tall in the mall?

The good news is that there are some things that will help you deal with issues like this. The first step is addressing the spiritual side, that stronghold, that makes you crave sexuality. However, next, before we deal with any practical things, we need to address the heart. Strongholds are clearly influencers, but so is the heart.

Your Heart
Jeremiah 17:9 has some pretty strong things to say about the heart.

> "The human heart is the most deceitful of all things, and desperately wicked. Who really knows how bad it is?"

And also Matthew 15:19-20,

> "For out of the heart come evil thoughts, murder, adultery, sexual immorality, theft, false witness, slander. These are what defile a person."

Our heart - pre-Jesus - doesn't do too much for us. Our heart desperately needs redemption and that only comes from one place. In Psalm 51:10, David knew the state of the human heart, his heart, and cried out,

"Create in me a clean heart, O God."

Since you have struggled with sexual immorality, how many times have you asked God to create in you a clean heart? The answer for me was never, at least not that I can remember. It wasn't until I addressed the strongholds where that drive to sin originated that I could understand that, and once I dealt with the spiritual side and it was taken care of, I realized that I also needed a change in my heart. It was like the stronghold deceived my heart, and they were working together to radiate sinfulness within me. My heart was literally working against me! Addressing the heart is incredibly important because in Proverbs 4:23, the Bible tells us,

> "Guard your heart above all else, for it determines the course of your life."

Other translations say "out of your heart issue the springs of life." I want you to imagine that for a moment. Your heart determines your course. Consider the scenario of walking in the mall and looking over to see giant photos of beautiful women in nothing but skimpy lace. Where your heart is in this fight is going to determine how you respond, and your response is key because it reveals just what is in your heart.

A heart that is pure before the Lord refuses to notice those posters, refuses to look, and refuses to allow the enemy to have a foothold. But a heart that is not pure, one that is not clean, will take you on a course that leads to sin, via the paths of lust, sexual fantasies, etc. You could look at those posters and think nothing of it in that moment, but late at night when you are all alone, the enemy flashes those images across your mind. Remember, he is sneaky and deceptive, always opting for the attack when you're least expecting it. An unclean heart follows the trail to sin, but a clean heart, because it had refused to allow the enemy a chance during the day, is harder to sway at night.

Your heart plays a huge role in this. Perhaps right now you should pause and ask God to purify your heart. Perhaps you have gotten so far into this lifestyle that you feel like your heart is as solid as a stone and it could never be clean. Then you need Ezekiel 36:26:

> "And I will give you a new heart, and a new spirit I will put within you. And I will remove the heart of stone from your flesh and give you a heart of flesh."

Praying this prayer is very simple. Just ask God to renew your heart.

> "God, I ask you to cleanse my heart. Purify my heart, Father. Search my heart. Test it. If there is anything unclean in it I am asking you to purify it. God, I give you permission to cleanse my heart. Father, I know what comes out of an unclean heart defiles a person. I want a pure heart, a clean heart, and I ask you to do that now. Thank you father for your faithfulness. Thank you for cleansing my heart. In Jesus' name, Amen."

Don't underestimate how important your heart is in this process. Now that it is clean, let's keep it that way. To do that, we'll talk about some incredible practical tools that will help you along the way in the next chapter.

CHAPTER 5

THE REQUIRED TOOLS

You are going to need to take advantage of some tools that God has given us to overcome the habitual sin in your life. These tools are life-changing and are specifically designed by God to give you what you need to live the life he has called you to live.

First we'll talk about tools that are required. When I say required, I simply mean that without these tools active in your life and without you using them every day, it will be impossible to overcome.

After 15+ years of counseling with people, and after dealing with my own struggles, I can tell you, without hesitation, that most failures are not due to outside stimuli, but are based on the fact that the Christian was severely weakened, and sometimes even crippled, by the lack of these tools, or by the fact the tools were not used. You can't hope to live the life God has created you for without them. They are that important! It is the difference between spiritual life and death.

1. Renewing Your Mind
We already addressed this earlier, but it is worth mentioning again, as it is so important in your freedom from sin.

Romans 12:1-2 tells us,

> "I appeal to you therefore, brothers, by the mercies of God, to present your bodies as a living sacrifice, holy and acceptable to God, which is your spiritual worship. Do not be conformed to this world, but be transformed by the renewal of your mind, that by testing you may discern what is the will of God, what is good and acceptable and perfect."

In this passage we see the benefits of renewing your mind, and that is that you can discern what is the will of God, what is good and acceptable and perfect. In Romans 8:5-6, we see how the mind plays a part in our walk with God.

> "For those who live according to the flesh set their minds on the things of the flesh, but those who live according to the Spirit set their minds on the things of the Spirit. For to set the mind on the flesh is death, but to set the mind on the Spirit is life and peace."

Where you put your thoughts pays a huge role in your outcome. Thinking on things of the flesh nets death, on the things of the Spirit, life. You may want to decide right now whether or not you want to live or die.

I'll give you a minute to decide.

Ok so you want to live. Great! Then you need to renew your mind. Every day. Once in the morning when you first wake up. Do it again each time you feel tempted. Do it again when you see something you shouldn't see. Renew it constantly. You can never do that enough.

Please understand that you, as a human, have a brain that was specifically designed by God to remember things. I don't want to spend too much time on the neurological functions and purposes of the brain, especially since I am a pastor, not a neurosurgeon, but it was made to remember. Sure it runs your organs, etc., but it only does that because it remembers to do it. Feel your pulse? Your brain remembered to send a signal to tell your physical heart to beat. #TheMoreYouKnow

Your brain is made to remember, and one of the things most people who have had sexual immorality in their past struggle with is remembering. They remember things they have seen. They remember porn they've seen online. They remember sexual experiences they've had with other people, kind of like a highlight reel. You can't help but remember situations, circumstances, environments, activities, and yes, images, videos, and reliving moments in your mind. I can hear a song and all of the sudden, it feels like I am back in time at a certain point. I remember the feelings I had, the environment, I sometimes remember the smells and the sensations. The mind remembers like it was made to do, and that can prove to be a huge obstacle to getting you free from sin.

But there is great news! While the mind was built to remember, God can do anything, even to wipe those memories away. In fact, an amazing ability that God has is the ability to forget. Consider Hebrews 8:12.

> "And I will forgive their wickedness, and I will never again remember their sins."

The writer of Hebrews is quoting Jeremiah, reinforcing the fact that God has the ability to forget our sins. How awesome is that? The Bible also tells us in 1 John 1:9,

> "But if we confess our sins to him, he is faithful and just to forgive us our sins and to cleanse us from all wickedness."

Once we confess our sin, he casts that sin into the sea (Mic 7:19). He does it for his own sake! (See Is. 43:25). If God can do that for himself, he can do it for us as well. You can take a moment to ask him to purify your mind. Ask him to cleanse your thoughts. Ask him to renew your mind. Ask him to delete those experiences, actions, thoughts, images, videos, etc.

I'll give you a minute.

Now that you have done that, it is important to continually renew your mind, every single day. Go back to chapter two if necessary and re-read the portion on renewing your mind. If you are going to defeat the enemy and keep him defeated, you are going to have to do this every day. It is not an option.

2. Prayer

I have been married since 2007 and there is one thing I can say is at the top of the list to have a successful marriage: communication. It is amazing how things crumble when communication is weak. If I expect to have a successful marriage, I had better learn to communicate often. But I also need to communicate well. It is not enough to just say words, I need to make sure that the communication leads to a deeper relationship with my wife.

You may not be married right now, but the illustration works for God as well. If you are going to have a relationship with God that means something, then you are going to have to communicate with him. And often. And on top of that, to communicate well.

If your prayer life is limited to meals and crises, how in the world do you expect to have a relationship with God that makes a difference? This type of prayer life isn't directed towards a God it is directed towards a genie. You may have even asked God to fix this problem of sexual immorality. You may have even gotten frustrated that he didn't fold his arms, nod his head, and fix all of your problems. I hate to be the bearer of bad news, but God doesn't wave wands. There is a process whereby issues have to be handled and handled thoroughly.

Most people couldn't handle the money if they won the lottery. In fact, there have been studies of people who have won the lottery and within a few years are more broke than they were before they won. This is the main reason why God won't snap his finger to make it all go away. If he did that, then you would never learn how to handle the attacks of the enemy that come daily.

You have got to learn to pray. You have got to schedule time every day to get before God, talk to him, tell him your concerns, your fears, your troubles, to praise him, to thank him, to honor him, and - I know this is revolutionary - to listen to him speak to you. If you are trying to fight the sexual immorality battle without a daily prayer time, you are walking into a battle in a bathrobe instead of armor. How in the world can you expect to live victoriously though Jesus Christ and the Holy Spirit if you never talk to God?

> **If you are trying to fight the sexual immorality battle without a daily prayer time, you are walking into a battle in a bathrobe instead of armor.**

The problem is that most people feel like prayer in the morning is either too time consuming, to awkward, or too hard. Let me ask you this: how much time have you spent feeling guilty about sinning sexually? Or how awkward was that moment the Sunday after you failed yet again, and you had to interact with God? How hard has not looking at porn been to you? Most people think they don't have the time to pray or the words to say. I'm telling you that you cannot afford not to pray.

Matthew 26:41 should resound in our minds when we think of prayer.

> "Watch and pray that you may not enter into temptation. The spirit indeed is willing, but the flesh is weak."

We have the watching down, but do you realize the massive role that prayer plays in your ability to avoid temptation? Why is that so? Because your spirit is willing but your flesh is weak. Your flesh doesn't want you to pray. It wants another 30 minutes in bed. It wants to stay up and watch tv. It wants you to click that link. But your spirit is yearning to connect with God, longing for that interaction. Your flesh has no will power, but your spirit is strong. But too often we ignore our spirit and walk in our flesh and then have the nerve to wonder why we failed. I don't mean to sound harsh, but the fact of the matter is that a prayer-less life is a sin-full life. What I mean by that is that when you are lacking in prayer, you are abundant in sin.

If you are struggling with sin, especially an habitual sin like sexual immorality, the quickest way to take a step towards victory is to start with prayer. It is necessary, whether you struggle with sin or not. If you consider yourself a Christian, prayer is simply necessary.

3. God's Word
Did you know that God's Word not only points us to him, reveals his character, and tells us how to be saved, but it also is one of the best ways to guard against sin, and it is filled with promises to help you live in constant victory? Almost too good to be true, but it is!

Of all the tools that God gives us to fight the enemy, the Word of God is the only offensive one. Everything else is defensive. Consider the Armor of God as found in Ephesians 6. Helmet, breastplate, shoes, shield. All provide protection from offense. The sword is unique in that it is both an offensive and defensive weapon. The sword can both deliver and block a blow. Isn't that interesting?

It should be to you, because the Bible calls the Sword of the Spirit the Word of God. Don't fail to recognize the importance of the Bible when it comes to overcoming sin. Other than the Holy Spirit, it is the best offensive weapon you have. The Word of God not only has the power to deflect the attack of the enemy, it has the power to slay the attacker!

Let's consider this scenario to illustrate the point.

You are at home in your bedroom. It has been a long day and you're tired. Kinda bored too. Earlier that day you went to the mall with some friends. All of the sudden, while you are remembering the day you had, you remember the girl that walked past you guys while you were eating in the Food Court. She was pretty. Really pretty. You begin to remember her hair, her walk, and then you remember her clothing choice. It left little to the imagination.

But at 10 pm laying in your bed, the enemy is happy to help you with that.

How do you respond? Use the Word of God. It will provide both amazing defense and a powerful offense.

"Thank you God that I am no longer a slave to sin (Romans 7)"

"Thank you that I have the mind of Christ (1 Cor. 2:16)."

"Thank you God that I am more than a conqueror through Christ Jesus (Romans 8:37)."

"Holy Spirit I ask you to help me renew my mind right now. (Romans 12:2)"

"I want to think upon things that honor you God. Holy Spirit help me now to think about things of the Spirit (Romans 8:5)."

It is pretty hard to think about a sexual fantasies when you are quoting Scripture. That's like making out on the altar. Super awkward. That is what God means when he says the spirit is willing but the flesh is weak. You see two massive contrasts here: the flesh that wants to dwell in a sinful fantasy, and the Spirit that is wanting you to be pure and holy. It is hard for the flesh to win when you are masterfully swinging the Sword of the Spirit.

Here's a neat trick if you want an extra boost. Many years ago while serving at a church in Jasper, Texas, one of the congregants, Millie, was praying scripture out loud. She always did that. So one day I asked her why she specifically prayed scripture out loud. Her response was life-changing.

"Well, Jason, because faith comes by hearing and hearing by the Word of God."

The moment she quoted Romans 10:17 to me, a lightbulb went off in my head. When I am tempted, I need faith to overcome. I need faith to activate the Holy Spirit to attack. I need faith in what God's Word tells me so that I can respond accurately and effectively. I may be using my physical mouth and vocal chords, but I am engaging a spiritual battle with a spiritual response. When I say those verses out loud, not only do I give myself the opportunity to be encouraged and strengthen by the Word of the Living God, I give the enemy the notice that his attacks will not succeed and that he is defeated. Praying those powerful verses out loud goes into my ears and builds faith, but it also goes into the enemy's ears and destroy his confidence in his attack and the work of his evil hands.

Praise God for his Word! If we would simply take advantage of the tools God gave us, especially his Word, we'd find that the temptations that come against us aren't as powerful as we once thought! What demon in hell can stand against God's Word? At what moment in history has God's Word ever been defeated by evil? The only time Christians are overrun by temptation and evil is when they refuse to stand and wield the Word of God like the sword it is, refusing to respond with built-up, bulldog faith in the face of temptation.

I don't care how pretty that girl was at the mall. It wouldn't matter if she were walking down the aisle in her birthday suit. You start speaking the Word of God in that moment and you can experience the power of the Holy Spirit charging in and destroying the battle lines of the enemy before your very eyes. It is pretty hard to lust after that girl when you are speaking the Word of God.

Maybe it wasn't a girl at the mall, but an image on the internet. Even a Google image search for "Jesus" will give nudity in the results. Whether it is a person or a click, the principle works the same way. Speak the Word of God and watch the temptation run like the coward it is.

Learn what the Bible says. Read it. Digest it. Get it in you every single day. If you don't want to sin against God, you need to hide his Word in your heart.

To help you learn some of these power verses to overcome temptation when it rises, I have included a list here. Learn these verses. Recite them often. Say them out loud if you need to. To general rule is recite them until you are free, and then ten more times!

> 1 Corinthians 10:13
> "The temptations in your life are no different from what others experience. And God is faithful. He will not allow the temptation to be more than you can stand. When you are tempted, he will show you a way out so that you can endure."
>
> James 4:7
> "So humble yourselves before God. Resist the devil, and he will flee from you."
>
> Romans 8:9
> "But you are not controlled by your sinful nature. You are controlled by the Spirit if you have the Spirit of God living in you."

Psalm 119:9-11
"How can a young person stay pure? By obeying your word. I have tried hard to find you—don't let me wander from your commands. I have hidden your word in my heart, that I might not sin against you."

Romans 8:12-13
"You have no obligation to do what your sinful nature urges you to do. For if you live by its dictates, you will die. But if through the power of the Spirit you put to death the deeds of your sinful nature, you will live."

Romans 6:12-13
"Do not let sin control the way you live; do not give in to sinful desires. Do not let any part of your body become an instrument of evil to serve sin. Instead, give yourselves completely to God, for you were dead, but now you have new life. So use your whole body as an instrument to do what is right for the glory of God."

Romans 8:26-27
"And the Holy Spirit helps us in our weakness. For example, we don't know what God wants us to pray for. But the Holy Spirit prays for us with groanings that cannot be expressed in words. And the Father who knows all hearts knows what the Spirit is saying, for the Spirit pleads for us believers in harmony with God's own will."

Romans 12:1-2
"And so, dear brothers and sisters, I plead with you to give your bodies to God because of all he has done for you. Let them be a living and holy sacrifice—the kind he will find acceptable. This is truly the way to worship him. Don't copy the behavior and customs of this world, but let God transform you into a new person by changing the way you think. Then you will learn to know God's will for you, which is good and pleasing and perfect."

Romans 8:31
"If God is for us, who can ever be against us?"

2 Corinthians 10:3-5
"We are human, but we don't wage war as humans do. We use God's mighty weapons, not worldly weapons, to knock down the strongholds of human reasoning and to destroy false arguments. We destroy every proud obstacle that keeps people from knowing God. We capture their rebellious thoughts and teach them to obey Christ."

2 Corinthians 12:7-10
"My grace is all you need. My power works best in weakness."

Ephesians 6:10-12
"A final word: Be strong in the Lord and in his mighty power. Put on all of God's armor so that you will be able to stand firm against all strategies of the devil. For we are not fighting against flesh-and-blood enemies, but against evil rulers and authorities of the unseen world, against mighty powers in this dark world, and against evil spirits in the heavenly places."

Philippians 4:8-13
"And now, dear brothers and sisters, one final thing. Fix your thoughts on what is true, and honorable, and right, and pure, and lovely, and admirable. Think about things that are excellent and worthy of praise. Keep putting into practice all you learned and received from me—everything you heard from me and saw me doing. Then the God of peace will be with you."

Colossians 3:1-5
"Since you have been raised to new life with Christ, set your sights on the realities of heaven, where Christ sits in the place of honor at God's right hand. Think about the things of heaven, not the things of earth. For you died to this life, and your real life is hidden with Christ in God. And when Christ, who is your life, is revealed to the whole world, you will share in all his glory. So put to death the sinful, earthly things lurking within you. Have nothing to do with sexual immorality, impurity, lust, and evil desires. Don't be greedy, for a greedy person is an idolater, worshiping the things of this world."

Hebrews 4:14-16
"So then, since we have a great High Priest who has entered heaven, Jesus the Son of God, let us hold firmly to what we believe. This High Priest of ours understands our weaknesses, for he faced all of the same testings we do, yet he did not sin. So let us come boldly to the throne of our gracious God. There we will receive his mercy, and we will find grace to help us when we need it most."

Hebrews 12:1-2
"Therefore, since we are surrounded by such a huge crowd of witnesses to the life of faith, let us strip off every weight that slows us down, especially the sin that so easily trips us up. And let us run with endurance the race God has set before us. We do this by keeping our eyes on Jesus, the champion who initiates and perfects our faith."

Philippians 4:13
"I can do all things through Jesus Christ who gives me strength."

Romans 8:37
"No, in all these things we are more than conquerors through him who loved us."

Isaiah 41:10
"Don't be afraid, for I am with you. Don't be discouraged, for I am your God. I will strengthen you and help you. I will hold you up with my victorious right hand."

Psalm 46:1
"God is our refuge and strength, always ready to help in times of trouble."

2 Timothy 1:7
"For God has not given us a spirit of fear and timidity, but of power, love, and self-discipline."

Zephaniah 3:17
"For the Lord your God is living among you. He is a mighty savior. He will take delight in you with gladness. With his love, he will calm all your fears. He will rejoice over you with joyful songs."

2 Corinthians 5:17
"Anyone who belongs to Christ has become a new person. The old life is gone; a new life has begun!"

Deuteronomy 31:6
"So be strong and courageous! Do not be afraid and do not panic before them. For the Lord your God will personally go ahead of you. He will neither fail you nor abandon you."

1 Corinthians 16:13
"Be on guard. Stand firm in the faith. Be courageous. Be strong."

So how does this work? You simply pray these verses over you.

"God I know that you have made me more than a conqueror through Jesus Christ, so right now I conquer the thoughts that are attacking me right now. I am a new creation. I am not weak, but strong and I know that, through you Jesus, I can do anything."

There are so many more verses, but that's a great start. Find those verses that really move and encourage you. Get into the Word. Listen to the Holy Spirit speak to you though God's Word. And remember that the Word of God is an amazing and powerful weapon God has given us in this fight!

These are some things (1. Renewing Your Mind, 2. Prayer, and 3. God's Word) that are required things you need to do on a daily basis.

Authority
Before we get away from this point about the Word of God, let me mention the fact that you, as a child of God, have been given authority over the power of the enemy. In Luke 10, Jesus sent out 72 disciples to preach the Kingdom of God. This included overcoming the power of the enemy. When the 72 returned, they were amazed that "even the demons obey us when we use your name." Jesus responded to their excitement in verses 19-20.

> "Look, I have given you authority over all the power of the enemy, and you can walk among snakes and scorpions and crush them. Nothing will injure you. But don't rejoice because evil spirits obey you; rejoice because your names are registered in heaven."

> **As a child of God, you have been given authority over the power of the enemy.**

If you have asked Jesus Christ to be Lord of your life, then an entry has been added to the registry of names in heaven, and that means you qualify for this authority over the power of the enemy! So how does that work?

When the enemy attacks you, you need to understand that, first you are no longer a slave to sin, which means you are under no obligation to obey, but second, you have the authority to address the enemy, to rebuke his attack, and to command him to leave. The enemy won't be obeying your authority, but the authority that comes with the fact that you belong to Jesus Christ.

The passage mentions snakes and scorpions. That is a metaphor. Consider how snakes and scorpions attack: snakes are sneaky, they are hidden, they lurk in the shadows and wait for a moment to attack. Scorpions may fight you head on, but they kill with a back-end blow the you aren't expecting. Doesn't that sound like how sexual immorality works? It sneaks upon you when you aren't expecting it. It waits for the moment of weakness to pounce.

Friend, you, in the name of Jesus, have authority over the power of the enemy. That is why we say, "In Jesus' name" at the end of a prayer. That is why, when the enemy attacks, you can rebuke him and command him to leave.

> "In the name of Jesus, I rebuke the attack of the enemy against me right now. By the authority that I have received through Jesus Christ, I command the enemy to leave and every attack against me right now to stop. In the name of Jesus, Amen."

The name of Jesus has immense power, and as a child of God, Jesus Christ has given you the authority to use his name over the power of the enemy. It is another tool in your belt, and I promise that if you will use it, you will give the same report as the 72 that "even the demons obey us when we use your name."

With that being said, I would like to add one more to the required list, and while you won't do this every day, you need to do this multiple times a week.

4. Get Connected with a Healthy, Life-Giving Local Church
Jesus Christ is no doubt the answer for the world today, but the local church is the way he is getting that answer to humanity. Not only that, the local church is an unbelievably effective tool to use in order to overcome habitual sin in your life. How? Glad you asked.

In Genesis 2, Moses had finished telling us about the creation of the world in 6 days, how the heavens and earth were formed, plants, creatures, how it all came to be. By this time, God had created man and had placed him in the Garden of Eden. God had also given him a job. But then, God makes an incredible statement to the hosts of Heaven in Genesis 2:18.

> "It is not good for man to be alone."

With that one statement, God revealed a truth about human beings, that it is not good for us to be alone. In fact, God never intended for anyone to ever be alone. He created us to find joy in relationships, to find peace in communing with others, and to find strength in the presence of God and his people. Even lost people have within them a desire for relationship. Deep within us is the need for relationship. We all want to be loved. We all want to be accepted. We all want to experience relationships with other people that are fulfilling. And while these reasons are awesome, and quite frankly, enough, God had another reason that he made us with a pre-installed need for relationships:

God knew we were going to need help from time to time.

I don't know if you knew this, but church is not for God. It is for you. Church gives you the opportunity to come together and worship and learn and grow. You can praise God anywhere. Psalm 139:7-8 tells us,

> "I can never escape from your Spirit! I can never get away from your presence! If I go up to heaven, you are there; if I go down to the grave, you are there."

Where can we go where God is not there? He is always near and because he is always near, a building is not a prerequisite to worshiping him. Plus, in the day and age we live in, you can click on television or download a podcast to hear a sermon. You can stream them online live and watch like you are there. All of these are great tools to help reach the lost and learn more about God, but again, these things are not for God. They are for you. But if you neglect regular attendance in a local truth-teaching church, you are missing out on a huge part of the whole reason it exists.

Hebrews 10:25 is pretty clear about this.

> "And let us not neglect our meeting together, as some people do, but encourage one another, especially now that the day of his return is drawing near."

If you miss out on church, then you are missing out on the fullness that God has for you. In fact, you are going to miss out on some things that he says to you, because some things he says are to the church and the church alone. Check out the first three chapters of Revelation and find out what I mean. Sometimes the word he speaks is for the body, not the individual. You need to be in church. It has nothing to do with offering plates or attendance. It has to do with your ability to grow in the Lord, encourage others, and be encouraged when you need it.

I don't know how you live, but I am not on cloud nine every day. There are some days when I struggle. Some days I feel like charging hell with a water pistol, but other days, I feel like I got punched in the face by a demonic chimpanzee. Not every day the sun is shining and the birds are singing, but that is the infinite beauty of getting involved in a local church.

On those days when I am king of the world, I can encourage and build up others. I can pray and love and speak life into my brothers and sisters. But on those days when I am low, I need - desperately need - my brothers and sisters to speak life into me! I need to hear, "Hey man, I am praying for you." "Hey brother, hang in there." "Hey brother, I want you to know you aren't alone. I am going to walk through this with you. I am going to be by your side. And when you start to lean to the left or to the right, I will stand by your side and hold you up until you can stand on your own."

THAT'S what church is about. Church helps you be better, be stronger, love harder, pray more powerfully, encourage more fervently, and be strengthened when you need it. That is why church is under the mandatory section. And especially when you are walking through deliverance from years of sexual immorality and habitual sin, you need some people in your life who believe the best about you and are dedicated to seeing you win. You need people who have your best interests in mind and are ready to go to battle on your behalf. You won't find that at the therapist's office, but you will at God's house.

I know people have bad experiences with church people sometimes. I get that. It is sad, but there are broken people at church too. But don't let a few bad apples spoil the basket. If you are in a place full of bad apples, maybe you need to pray about finding a new basket. I'm not telling you to leave a church, but it is God's will for your life to be engaged in a truth-teaching, Spirit-led local church. Let him guide you in that.

The bottom line is that you need to have a place, a safe place, where you can live life with people and build trust and respect, and if you are struggling with an issue, to pull them aside and tell them, "Hey man I am struggling and I don't want to struggle anymore." Do you know how excited that makes God? Jesus Christ was the prime example of carrying another's burden, and when we do the same, the Bible says in Galatians 6 that we are "obeying the law of Christ." He loves it!

Church is not a drudgery or a chore. It is the place where you have the opportunity to learn how to be who God has called you to be. Freedom lives there. Hope lives there. Healing lives there. Encouragement lives there. Renew your mind, pray, read the Word, but don't neglect coming to church. You need these allies, your brothers and sisters in Christ, battle buddies willing to jump in the trench with you, to enrich your walk with God, and help you through when times get rough.

Now that we've hit these four areas that are required, let's talk about some tools you can use that will help you stay free. You don't have to use all of these, but figure out which tools can help you in your new pure life!

CHAPTER 6

THE PRACTICAL TOOLS

When I talk about practical tools, I am talking about resources that can help you overcome sin and honor God. These tools can be a variety of things, many of them are not even spiritual things. Let me give you some examples.

I love apps. I actually have apps that help me find apps. Don't judge me. One of my apps is Chase Bank. There's nothing spiritual about the Chase Bank app. It is a good app that works well, but there's nothing holy about it. However, I use it to manage my income. It helps me steward what God has provided for me. So in that sense, it is not necessarily spiritual, but it helps me honor God by keeping track of the money he provides.

I started using a new app called Slack. It is a communication app for people so they can stay in contact while working on projects, discussing business issues, etc. There's nothing holy or spiritual about it at all, but we are using it at church to communicate between our leadership so that we can have an open dialogue to spot issues, share wins, and better accomplish the task God has us doing. That is really awesome, and it helps us do what God has called us to better and more efficiently.

There are tools out there you can use that will help you stay free from sin. Some of these tools are spiritual, but some aren't at all. I've used a ton of different apps that did the same general thing, especially with budgeting/finance tracking apps, but I had to find the one that worked best for me. The same is true with these tools. They are all good and will help you, but you need to find the formula that works for you. Of course, there's only one catch, and the catch is the same for any tool, even my apps:

    You have to use them.

The Chase app, the Slack app, they never do anything for me if I never open them. But because I do, and because I put them to work, they help me. A lot. The song says love isn't love until you give it away. A tool isn't beneficial until you use it.

The truth is, you may find that not all of these tools will work just right for you. They all may, but some might not. That's no problem. But some of them will work for everyone. Would you just stop for a moment and commit to doing some of these? Purpose in your heart that you are going to glean from the wisdom that you are about to read and put these tools to use.

Let's start with the first one!

1. Accountability

Honestly, this one could really be number five in the Required Tools section, but if you are doing number four from that section properly (getting engaged with a local church), then accountability should not be an issue. So let me just say it straight up so there's no confusion.

You **need** people in your life to hold you accountable.

No cuts. No buts. No coconuts. You need accountability in your life. I am curious how well you are doing in answering to God if you are not willing to have anyone in your life you answer to. I don't mean you have a boss, per se, but we live in a world that is dying for Yes Men and is allergic to No Men. You need someone in your life who will say, "No." You need someone who you trust enough to walk up to you, in love and genuine concern, and say to you, "What you are doing is not healthy for you." Now this is hard for some people. People don't like to hear no, but let me ask you this: in your last failure, would you have rather liked to experience the pain that comes from failure or the uncomfortableness that comes from a "No" before the fact? If you answered "I'd rather have the pain," you might be a masochist. That would be an interesting twist to Jeff Foxworthy's act.

> You **need** people in your life to hold you accountable.

In the good 'ol U. S. of A., where the eagle flies and Old Glory waves, we don't like to be accountable. We want to be free and independent and live life on our terms. That may work for a nation (for a while), but it is not sustainable. Eventually, with no one to hold you to account, the only logical conclusion is destruction. Independence isn't a good thing in Christianity.

Chuck Warnock, Senior Pastor of New Covenant Church in Longview, Tx once said, "We confuse individuality with independence. God prizes individuality but not independence." Independence says, "I don't need anyone." Accountability says, "I don't need to do this on my own."

Accountability is not a sign of weakness, it is an evidence of wisdom. A vote for accountability is a vote for wise counsel and a desire to please God. You need this in your life, and I can almost guarantee you that if you would have had accountability in place - and used that accountability - you would have had a whole lot harder time failing.

So how do you find these accountability partners? Simple. Ask someone. Super hard, right? There are some traits you need to look for first:

1. **Choose overcomers.**
    Are they struggling with it too? If they are, they may not be the best choice as an accountability partner. If you need help with budgeting, don't go to the guy who can't even make ends meet. Build relationships. Be transparent. Those who have overcome will show themselves. If that process is too long, ask your pastor who can help you find someone to help you be accountable. Just ask!

2. **Choose your same gender.**
    If you are a guy, build relationships with other guys. If you are struggling with sexual immorality, don't have the opposite sex as your accountability partner. You are just asking for it with that setup.

3. **Choose those who have the time.**
    There are people out there who really want to help, but they are scheduled to the max and just don't have extra time to give. If that is the case, don't take it personally. Thank God, actually, that they love you enough to tell you. You need someone who is willing to meet with you, at the minimum, every other week. Any less than that and they really can't get a pulse on your progress.

4. **Choose a crew.**
    Sometimes, finding an accountability partner can be tough. That can be life sometimes. If you can't find someone to walk with you who has overcome this issue, get a band of peers - even if they are fighting the same battles - that you can stick with. Not just one person but a group of people. You guys may be going through the battle together, and though you don't have someone who has won it all just yet, you'd rather be in the battle with friends than there all alone.

There are no super heroes in Christianity. Jesus already took that spot. Find someone, or a group of people, who can walk with you. Find a mentor, a spiritual father, someone who has overcome your war, and get counsel from them. Be willing to say yes to a no. Be willing to listen and follow counsel. The following counsel part is super important. Unused advice is worthless.

The best part about the fight is knowing that with God, you can win. The second best part is knowing you don't have to be alone. Get some accountability.

2. Code Words
Now that we have established the need for accountability, code words are something you may want to consider. I am a huge advocate of code words and use them in my own life. Here's how that works.

Let's say I struggle with porn, but I am committed to overcoming the issue, and have enlisted a group of guys to help me be accountable. Now let's say it is late at night and I am alone and the devil comes knocking at my door, tempting me with looking at porn. I pull out my phone, but instead of opening Safari, I open iMessage and send a group text that says, "FOXTROT" to my boys. All of the sudden, I feel encouraged, I feel strengthened, because I know, at that precise moment, several other guys are praying for me, lifting me up, asking God to give me strength.

Seconds later, I get a text that says, "Start quoting your power verses out loud. Do it." Another that says, "Get up and go outside with your Bible and start reading Romans 8." Another that says, "Our Father promised a way of escape. Open your eyes. Where's the exit?" Now I am praying out loud. I am reading my Word. I have recognized and have taken the escape route. I no longer have that urge. The enemy is gone. I can go to sleep. My crew knew exactly what was happening.

All I sent was a code word, but that random word launched a series of missiles that destroyed the work of the enemy. You don't need a ton of faith in that moment. You just need enough faith to click the right icon. Powerful stuff.

Code words are great for many areas of your life. See how they can help you. Get creative!

3. Stops
There are some aspects of this battle that require you to establish stops, or boundaries for yourself. You know what you ought to do, so you just

need to do it. Alcoholics don't need to go to bars. Porn addicts don't need certain apps and accounts. You've got to use common sense in order to make some of these decisions, but perhaps you need clear boundaries when it comes to temptation.

Here is a list of things I recommend you do to stop the temptation:

1. **Get a family member involved in the solution.**
   If you tell someone in your family that you are struggling, you gain an advocate at home to help you stay free. I realize that not all families are like this, however, if you can get an advocate at home. They can make a world of difference.

2. **Only use your devices around other people.**
   Perhaps you need to establish a rule that you cannot be alone with your electronic device or computer. It is pretty difficult to look at bad stuff when you are sitting with other people in the room. #awkward

3. **No phones at night.**
   If looking at stuff on your phone at night is an issue, then establish a rule with your parents (if you're a teen) that your parents get your phone when you go to bed. Don't have your phone during that time period. It is hard to look at stuff online if you don't have the device that gets you online. If you are married, make sure your spouse has it. Tell him/her to hide it if they need to. Do what you have to do to stop the influence by barricading doors.

4. **No phones in the bathroom.**
   If you are going to send a naked photo or look at porn when people are at home, the odds are that you are going to do it in the bathroom. If you refuse to allow the phone in the bathroom with you, you eliminate the temptation.

   I know what you are thinking. "What am I going to do while I am in there." They make these things that are wrapped in leather and have tons of pages with tiny writing. They call it a Bible and it is this thing that you can read that will help you overcome sin. Pretty cool. And the best part is that it doesn't run out of battery halfway through your "Me" time on the toilet. Read your Bible. Even if you don't read your Bible in the bathroom, ten minutes of boredom is better than an eternity of hell (1 Cor. 6:9-10).

5. **Kill the apps.**
   We all know that there are those apps out there that are good for nothing but sinning. There are too many apps to list right now, but if you find that an app is too much of a temptation, delete it. Seriously. Here's how you know: If you use the app to sin, sexually or not, it is bad.

   Before you delete the app, if it requires a login, change your password. Here's what I suggest: type some random strain of text, then highlight and cut it, then change your password by pasting this new jumble of letters into the change password field. If you can't log back in, it makes it harder to fail. Even if you try to reset the password, you give yourself more time to allow the Holy Spirit to step in and for you to come to your senses.

   You need to ask yourself what is more important, not using an app or losing your soul. In fact, if you know what apps are causing you to struggle, delete them now. The next paragraph will be here when you get back. Do it now. You might not have the willpower to do it later. Go. Delete it!

6. **Get Tech help.**
   There are several apps out there that can help you deal with looking at immoral things online, both on your cellphone and computer. One great free resource is offered by the Triple X Church (xxxchurch.com), which is a church built around getting people free from sexual addiction. They offer an app called X3 Watch (x3watch.com). You simply disable your native web browser in your settings, and enable X3 Watch's web browser. If you look at anything questionable, or try to reenable Safari, it sends an email to your accountability immediately. It even sends a report each week of whether or not your failed or succeeded. XXX Church also offers a ton of resources on their website to help you stay free, including great blogs, powerful tools, and even online accountability groups.

   Another app like this that is a paid app is Covenant Eyes. I don't know a great deal about this app because I only used X3 Watch, but they offer a variety of tools the help you overcome this temptation. It is comparable to X3Watch Pro, which is XXX Church's paid version.

7. **Forget your passwords.**
   When it comes to your cellphone, I recommend having your

parent or accountability create your App/Play Store password for you. I have a friend once who did this and it worked well for him. He needed to do an update on his phone, but he couldn't because he didn't know the password. His friend called me, I put in the password, and he updated his phone. Was it an extra couple of steps? Yes. Was it a little more hassle? Yep. But he was never tempted with downloading something sketch either.

8. **Check your relationships.**
I don't know if you know this, but not everyone has your best interest in mind. Some people want to drag you down because that is where they are. You need to be wise enough to know what relationships are not good for you and which ones need to go.

If the person you are with is constantly trying to get you in bed, get rid of them. If all somebody asks you on Snapchat or Kik or text for a nude, drop them. You don't need that in your life. On a side note, you may need to drop Snapchat and Kik too. Remember anything that leads you into sin is not worth it. The negatives outweigh the positives.

By the way, evangelism dating is a bad idea. I'm so happy you "want them to get saved," but you need to understand that, first, you are not following God's command by not being unequally yoked (1 Cor. 6), and second, you are believing a lie that they won't bring you down. Don't take my word for it. Check out 1 Corinthians 15:33.

"Do not be deceived: 'Bad company ruins good morals.'"

And even beyond that point, don't you think God loves you enough to provide someone to marry who loves him and is committed to honoring him? Don't settle for who's available. Wait for who is right.

The best thing to say about all of these tools is just to be smart about what you are doing. You know if what you are doing is having a negative impact, then get rid of it. It isn't worth the sin. Never forget what James had to say in James 4:17.

"Remember, it is sin to know what you ought to do and then not do it."

Listen, I realize these can be hard. It is one thing to say, "Drop that guy or girl, " or "Delete the app, bruh" and another thing to do it. But this is a great chance to tell you that this is what accountability is for! These accountability partners in your life are dedicated to seeing you free. they can encourage you in how to break it off with that person you shouldn't be with. They can delete the apps for you. But at the end of the day, you have to make the decision whether or not you want to stay free. What is it going to be?

4. No Second Looks Principle
In Luke 11:34-36, we read a powerful verse about our vision.

> "Your eye is a lamp that provides light for your body. When your eye is good, your whole body is filled with light. But when it is bad, your body is filled with darkness. Make sure that the light you think you have is not actually darkness. If you are filled with light, with no dark corners, then your whole life will be radiant, as though a floodlight were filling you with light."

We've seriously got to be careful what our eyes see. *Be careful little eyes what you see!* It isn't just a kid's song. It is the truth! But let's be honest, you can't help what walks into your view. Now, if you decide to watch 50 Shades of Gray, then yes, you can help it, but if you are at the mall and you see Victoria telling her Secrets on the wall, there's not a lot you can do about it. Perhaps you could tell the mall manager that these are sexually explicit and ask they have them removed. I don't know if that would work or not. But the best course of action is to properly handle that first look.

That's where second looks comes in.

Something we do in our ministry here is called Second Mile, Second Nature. This is a philosophy that we learned from Gateway Students at Gateway Church in Southlake, Tx that we have adopted, and, I think they learned it from Chik-Fil-A. #nuggets

The whole principle is that we need to go the second mile with people. It came from Matthew 5 where Jesus told the people, "If a Roman soldier demands you carry his pack for a mile, carry it for two." In the first mile, the person is a slave, but in the second, they are free. It is an encouragement to go the extra mile, because, as Gateway puts it, "We believe life-change happens in the second mile." Beautiful concept. And it works!

I say all that to tell you that if life change happens in the second mile with the Second Mile, Second Nature principle, I want you to know that destruction comes with the second look in the No Second Looks principle.

You can't help what walks into your view, but you can help the second look. The moment I see those sketch posters, or a girl walks in front of me wearing nothing, there is a moment where the enemy tries to make me a slave again. But if I purpose in my heart that I refuse to take a second look, I refuse to allow the enemy to trap me, what I gain is my freedom back. In that moment, I destroy any foothold the enemy tried to take. The devil knocked on my door, but I refused to answer.

> You can't help what walks into your view, but you can help the second look.

Don't take second looks. But if you slip and do take one, repent right then! Ask for forgiveness! Ask the Holy Spirit to renew your mind right then! And if you really want to win, text your accountability and tell them you made a second look, and then be honest with how you responded. Again, you have to make the decision whether or not you want to stay free. What is it going to be?

All of these tools can help you overcome the temptation to sin, but again, I must reinforce the fact that there are spiritual battles that take place that you have to address, which I hope you have done now, and there are more battles on the horizon that you must overcome as well. I wish that the battle would just happen once and it would be over with, like a big test at school, but the enemy will not stop trying to destroy us until Jesus destroys him in the end.

The good news is that while the enemy himself is not yet destroyed, his power over you as a child of God, bought with the Blood of Jesus, is! Satan has no power over you, and the only influence he has in your life is the influence you allow him. Jesus has already defeated the enemy. It is high time you step into your rightful place as victor as well.

I do want to encourage you that while the battles will come, they will get easier to overcome. At first, the enemy is going to heighten the attack, so get ready for that, but the difference between then and now is that you are no longer fighting this battle with your natural, physical means. You are waging a new kind of war, one that is led by the Holy Spirit, and he is tearing down strongholds in your life! The battle may get more intense, but I promise that if you will stay the course, and continue to walk in the Spirit, you will begin to see each battle become easier to win. The closer you get the Jesus the further you get from sin. Rest in the fact that, if you will do what God asks, you will win. If you mean it, he means it. That is something to get excited about!

CHAPTER 7

QUESTIONS

I am often asked about different parts of the puzzle that is human sexuality, from pornography to sex acts to sexual intercourse and everything in between. People often have questions about everything from kissing to masturbation to homosexuality, etc., so I thought I might take a moment and answer some of the most common questions from a biblical standpoint.

1. Why is sex before marriage wrong?
Sex is something that is beautiful and powerful and was created by God. The world has really messed up something that was meant to be a super personal, intimate experience with your spouse. But that last part is the key: your spouse.

Anytime you engage in premarital sex, including sexual related activity (everything from kissing to "everything but"), you are using it out of its intended purpose. Track with me on this:

1. In terms of sexuality, God created man and woman for each other, for companionship and reproduction (Gen. 2)
2. The expectation is that you are a virgin when you marry (Deut. 22.)
3. In multiple passages, God warns us not to engage in sexual immorality. Each of these verses uses the Greek, *porneia*, which is translated into English as "illegitimate sexual intercourse," with illegitimate referring to sex outside of the bonds of marriage (1 Cor. 7:9. Also see Acts 15:20; Gal. 5:19; Eph. 5:3; 1 Thess. 4:3; Rev. 9:21).
4. God intended that sexual relationships be limited to the marital bed (1 Cor. 7:9, Heb. 13:5).

I find it very interesting that the Greek word, *porneia*, is literally translated as "selling off" (Strong's, 4202). The word has also been rendered as a way to define prostitution, which is a person "selling" their body for gain. When you have premarital sex, you are selling off a portion of what was meant for your spouse. You are taking resources, physical, emotional, spiritual, etc., that were destined for your spouse out of their storehouse and giving it to another. That is an amazing word picture right there. Really intense.

I have been very open in my life about my failures when it comes to sexual immorality and I can say, without question, my greatest regret is that I was not pure when I got married. Standing on that altar, my wife could give me that, but I could not give it to her. I had carelessly and recklessly sold off what was meant for her to others. That is heartbreak, friends.

But you don't have to experience the same fate! And even if you have, God is a God of restoration and he can mend and replace that with which you have been careless. Sex is meant for the marriage bed. Sexual acts are meant for the marriage bed. That is a part of why Hebrews 13:4 says the marriage bed is undefiled.

Bottom line, sex is for marriage and marriage alone. Any expression of sexuality outside of the covenant of marriage is not pleasing to God, and, according to the Bible, sinful.

2. What about other sexual acts, like oral sex, etc?
A question like this is typically asked in order to figure out the boundary line so the asker can get as close to it as possible. Let me just answer this question with a question:

Are you married?

If you answered no, then I will refer you back to the first question. Any sexual act outside of marriage is immoral.

If you answered yes, then I'd like to offer you a great list to go by from Marriage Today founder, Jimmy Evans, which he posted at marriagetoday.com.

> "When it comes to the question of whether to allow or disallow any sexual practice, I recommend asking these questions:
>
> - Is it forbidden in the Bible?
> - Does it violate my conscience before God?
> - Does it violate my spouse or is it against his or her will?
> - Is it physically safe? Does it cause harm to me or my spouse? Are there health issues or risks involved?

- Does this treat my spouse in a disrespectful manner or damage our relationship in any way?"

3. Is kissing bad?
First let me ask what is the purpose of kissing? Most people kiss, initially, to see whether or not they have that "spark." While I guess that is an excuse, it is a really bad one. If you have to kiss someone to figure out if they are for you or not, you are not using a godly measuring tool. Beyond that, you should consider what that act initiates in your mind. I don't know about you, but I have never kissed a person in a romantic fashion and not thought about the next step. Why? Because kissing is the first step that is designed to lead to the next step. It simply opens doors to other things that are not healthy for you.

In two different places in the Old Testament book Song of Solomon, the writer says not to awaken love before its proper time (2:7. 8:4). If you are not to awaken love, what is the purpose of kissing? It's like putting your phone on the edge of the bathtub. You know your phone is about to play submarine. You are setting yourself up for failure.

4. Should I date, then?
In my opinion, you should only date when marriage is the end result. I used to be a huge advocate for dating. "Date! It is fun! Dating even helps you figure out the kind of person you want to be with." Lies. You can have fun and decide what personality types you like without dating. So many people think that the only thing that dating does is that it provides companionship. They don't see the connection, however, to the other door it opens, which is sexual immorality.

Think back to the first question. Why did God create Eve? Companionship and reproduction. That is what he intended from the romantic/marital relationship, and those two things go together hand in hand. So why then do we think we can have a dating relationship and utilize only the companionship part? Just like with God, you can't just have truth, and you can't just have spirit, you must have them both (John 4:24). They are inseparable. The same is true with companionship and reproduction. Don't believe the lie that you can just date and nothing else. Even if you don't have sex, I guarantee you've thought of it. How could you not?

5. What about masturbation? Is it sin?
I have had a lot of questions about this specific item and typically break down the answer into two parts: what the Bible says, and what the action does. Let's start by talking about what the Bible says.

The Bible never says, "Thou shall not masturbate nor touch thyself in any way," so if you are looking for that passage, you will not find it. However, the Bible does reference an act that most scholars agree describes the act of masturbation and the response to the act. This reference is found in Leviticus 15:16-17.

> "Whenever a man has an emission of semen, he must bathe his entire body in water, and he will remain ceremonially unclean until the next evening. Any clothing or leather with semen on it must be washed in water, and it will remain unclean until evening."

The Bible tells us that a man who has had an issue of semen is unclean until the next evening. First, we have to define unclean. In the context of Leviticus, unclean was a designation for someone or something that was disqualified from the ritual of corporate worship. While we see a connection in the Scriptures between being clean and holy, being unclean and unholy, that connection wasn't for every single case. In Leviticus 15:19, the Bible says that a woman in her time of menstruation is unclean as well. It is not a woman's sin that made her have a period. It is how female human biology works. In this case, she is not unclean due to sin, but simply due to a bodily function.

In verse 18 of the same chapter, we also see that sexual intercourse renders a couple unclean. The text doesn't specify if it is premarital or within the bonds of marriage, but since we know where God stands on premarital sex, the logical conclusion is that this passage is speaking of a man and woman within a marriage. God is clearly for sex between a man and his wife since he literally commanded them to reproduce in Genesis 1. God wasn't talking to the Stork Baby Delivery Company. So if God endorses sexual relations between a husband and wife, how could they be considered unclean or sinful? They aren't. But during this time, there were very specific laws about ceremonial worship and any bodily discharge, sexual or not, rendered you unclean. That included masturbation.

So am I saying masturbation is okay? Not so fast. There is nothing in the Bible that says masturbation is a sin. BUT - remember I said there were two parts here. Let's look at the second part, which is what the act does.

When a person masturbates, what are they thinking about? That, to me is the issue, and that is where the sin comes in.

Look at Matthew 5:27-28. This is Jesus talking about adultery.

> "You have heard the commandment that says, 'You must not commit adultery.' But I say, anyone who even looks at a woman with lust has already committed adultery with her in his heart."

Note Jesus didn't say that adultery was just the act itself, but even the thought of the act. Whenever a person engages in masturbation, there is nothing else for the mind to at that moment than to play out a sexual fantasy. In that moment, as your body responds physiologically to the stimuli, lust takes over in your mind, and you play out a scenario that eventually leads to the completion of that physical act. You would make a strong case in saying that masturbation in itself is not sinful according to the Bible, but you cannot overlook the fact that when you masturbate, your mind is flying down a trail that leads you into sin.

For this reason I say that masturbation is sinful. Not necessarily because the Bible calls it a sin, which it doesn't, per se, but because it opens a door for lust to enter, supplying a foothold for the enemy.

6. Is homosexuality wrong?
Yes. Plain and simple. In both the Old Testament and New, the Bible teaches that it is an abomination to God. Let's talk about why.

The bottom line is that homosexuality is against God's intended plan for sex. God clearly intended sexual relationships to provide enjoyment in marriage and reproduction. Yet beyond joy and reproduction, he made the man and woman to compliment each other, physically. This is how he intends sexual relationships and is how we should use sexual relationships.

In Romans 1:21-28, Paul speaks of homosexuality and connects it to the perverting of God's purpose.

> "Yes, they knew God, but they wouldn't worship him as God or even give him thanks. And they began to think up foolish ideas of what God was like. As a result, their minds became dark and confused. Claiming to be wise, they instead became utter fools. And instead of worshiping the glorious, ever-living God, they worshiped idols made to look like mere people and birds and animals and reptiles.
>
> So God abandoned them to do whatever shameful things their hearts desired. As a result, they did vile and degrading things with each

other's bodies. They traded the truth about God for a lie. So they worshiped and served the things God created instead of the Creator himself, who is worthy of eternal praise! Amen. that is why God abandoned them to their shameful desires. Even the women turned against the natural way to have sex and instead indulged in sex with each other. And the men, instead of having normal sexual relations with women, burned with lust for each other. Men did shameful things with other men, and as a result of this sin, they suffered within themselves the penalty they deserved.

Since they thought it foolish to acknowledge God, he abandoned them to their foolish thinking and let them do things that should never be done."

God's plan for sexuality between humans only included men with women and visa versa. God's plan never made allowance for same-sex intercourse because that was not a part of the plan. Some may find that difficult to digest, however, this "intended purpose" principle is evident in many other Christian doctrines, such as the fact that Jesus is the only way to Heaven, which counters pluralism, that salvation is based on grace, not works, which counters the idea that you can earn salvation, and even this issue of sex before marriage. So many people think the prerequisite for sexual relations is love. That simply is not what the Bible teaches. No matter what the culture teaches, it cannot trump what the Bible teaches.

> No matter what the culture teaches, it cannot trump what the Bible teaches.

Over and over again we find instances in the Bible where God has established an order, a rule, or a way, and humanity has chosen to act according to their own desires. No matter how diligently you argue the point, the Bible is crystal clear on the issue of homosexuality. It is against his plan, it is ungodly, and it is an abomination to him. This is arguably the most hotly contested issue in our culture today, yet it is one aspect of the Bible that is the most clear. That doesn't mean you bash homosexuals and scream they are going to hell. Yet believing the biblical teachings about homosexuality doesn't mean you are a homophobe either.

While this list is by no means comprehensive, these are some of the most often asked questions. These questions are legitimate and need addressing, but I would hate for you to see the answers and to think that God doesn't want you to have fun. We have to understand, however, what God's idea of fun really is. He delights in holiness and purity. He made you for those things, and when we are living for Jesus Christ, that's when we really experience the most fun.

The truth is, God loves you too much to let you fall into these sins like sexual immorality. Hebrews 11 talks about the "fleeting pleasures of sin." Any joy that comes from sin can only last a season. It is like an energy drink. You may feel pumped while you're on it, but you crash hard. Sin is the same, and God loves you too much to let you chug a can of sexual immorality only to crash once it is all done. That's why he is so dedicated to providing tools to overcome.

In our culture today, all we hear is that God is love. It is the only portion of Christian doctrine that everyone seems to agree on. People love the idea of a loving God, but not a God that addresses sin. They see a massive disconnect from love and discipline, love and conviction. Proverbs 13:24 addresses this disconnect.

> "Those who spare the rod of discipline hate their children. Those who love their children care enough to discipline them."

Godly discipline is a matter of love, not frustration with sin. What people need to understand is that God's discipline is not a reaction to his displeasure, but the evidence that God loves them. Hebrews 12:8 reinforces this.

> "If God doesn't discipline you as he does all of his children, it means that you are illegitimate and are not really his children at all."

This passage should illustrate completely why there is this disconnect between God's love and discipline in their minds. Those who can't unite those two, according to the text, are illegitimate and not really God's children!

The truth is, God **is** love, without any doubt. God doesn't just love, he is love, and you can know that he really loves you in that his loves is offered to you whether you are in agreement with his Word and ways or not. The issue should never be if he loves us (Rom. 5:8, Rom. 8), but how he loves us. Here's how deeply he does us: that he refuses to leave us where his love found us. God created us, he has a plan for us, and he knows us better than we know ourselves, and he knows that what he has planned for us is best. This is why God is willing to work sin out of your life. His love is determined to see us free!

That plan does not include addictions. It does not include rampant sin. It does not include immorality, and you definitely don't have to go through hell just to learn a lesson. But if you find yourself struggling with sexual sin, or any sin for that matter, you need to know that God's desire for you is freedom, it is liberty, it is restoration, and these things are possible!

These are great questions, and God has provided some very real answers. Now you have to decide what to believe. Now you have to make the choice whether or not you choose God's way or your own. I pray you choose God's way as it leads to life and liberty.

CHAPTER 8

FREEDOM

Even though it is often hostile and strenuous, there is something that is very sweet that comes from a battle, and that is the taste of victory once it is over. Listen, you are more than a conqueror. You are an overcomer. You are destined for victory. I don't care how far down the wrong trail you have gone. You are never too far where God can't reach you.

Trust in God to deliver you from this sin. I know right now it may seem that the battle is looming so largely in your life, but God is greater! He is mightier! Greater is he that is in you than he who is in the world! If you will follow his battle plan, you will win.

I pray that you have learned some things that will help deliver you from this sin. I also pray that you have learned some ways to stay free. But before the last word is written, I want to give you the opportunity to walk through the process of *confession*, *repentance*, *renouncing*, and finally *freedom*. It is not some magic formula. It is not hard. You just need to be honest with God, confess, repent, renounce, and receive his freedom.

God will forgive you and deliver you. God is faithful to do what he said he would do, and if you are ready to be cleansed, follow these steps.

Confession
Sexual immorality includes, among many other sins/strongholds/spirits, lust, sexual addiction, pornography, homosexuality, adultery, fornication, etc., and are sin. It is not the path God intended for you. You need to acknowledge that these are all sin, and because they are sin, they need to be confessed. 1 John 1:9 tells us,

> "But if we confess our sins to him, he is faithful and just to forgive us our sins and to cleanse us from all wickedness."

Confession is telling God what you have done. We've already established that God is all-knowing, so it may seem redundant to tell God what he already knows. I am not so sure confession is so God can know, rather so you can know. Something happens when you hear yourself confessing

> "If we confess our sins, he is faithful and just to forgive us our sins and to cleanse us from all wickedness."
>
> 1 John 1:9

your sin. Weight is lifted off your chest. Freedom - even at the moment of confession - begins to flow into your life.

I want to give you the opportunity to write down what you are going to confess to God. I asked you in an earlier chapter to write down the strongholds you believed were holding you down. Include these as well, but be sure to list everything you have engaged in so that you can confess it. You need freedom in every area, not just the big ones. If you have looked at porn, write it down. If you have looked at porn that is homosexual, involves some strange fetish, even beastiality or incest, write it down. Don't leave anything out. If you are having trouble, ask the Holy Spirit to bring to your mind what you need to confess. Write down any sin that he brings to your mind that you need to confess. As this book is about sexual immorality, I would ask you to write sins associated with that, however, you may have looked at pornography that is violent and want to confess anger. Whatever it is, write it down.

If you have engaged in physical sexual activity, like full on sex, write down those sins as well. The whole point is not to show your cards but to get freedom. You cannot get free until you are willing to confess everything, every act, every sin that has ensnared you. This may take time, and that is perfectly okay, so be thorough because it is worth it, I promise.

_____   _____
_____   _____
_____   _____
_____   _____
_____   _____
_____   _____
_____   _____
_____   _____
_____   _____
_____   _____
_____   _____
_____   _____
_____   _____
_____   _____

Now that you have written these things down, I am going to ask you to simply confess them. Go one by one and confess. It will sound something like this:

> "Father, I confess I have been lustful. I confess I have engaged in homosexual activity by watching pornography. I confess that I have had impure thoughts and have entertained sexual fantasies. I confess I have had sex outside of the covenant of marriage. I confess I have allowed my flesh to rule me. I confess I have engaged in viewing porn that depicts…etc."

Go down the line and confess them all. Once you have confessed them all, ask God to show you anything else you've missed. If there is anything, he will begin to bring it to your mind. Confess those things he brings to your mind.

Now that you have confessed, complete the confession by acknowledging that all these things are sin. It may go something like this:

> "Father, to my knowledge, I have confessed everything to you just now, and I acknowledge them all as sin. They are not your plan for me. By my own desire and actions, and in some situations by circumstance, I have allowed these sins, these strongholds, these spirits, to overcome me. I also acknowledge that there may be things that I haven't recognized that displease you. If there is anything that is in me that is displeasing to you, Father I acknowledge it as sin."

Repentance
Your next step is to repent of these sins. Let's be clear, repentance is not, "I'm sorry." It is "I'm sorry and I commit to never doing this again." Repentance is not asking for forgiveness, knowing that you are going to do it again. Repentance is turning and walking away from the sin.

Perhaps you have asked for forgiveness a thousand times. I can relate. At some point you desperately want the "I'm sorry" to be the last one. Let that be this one. Repentance isn't possible when strongholds are still in place, however, you have confessed those strongholds and destroyed them by the power of the Holy Spirit. That means your "I'm sorry" today has the power to stand. If you are ready, just say this prayer out loud, and mean it. Let the Holy Spirit do a work in you to keep you from returning to these sins.

> "Father I have confessed the sins that could think of that have held me captive to sexual immorality. I am asking for mercy. Please forgive

me. I don't blame anyone or anything else. I have committed these sins. I take responsibility for all of them. I ask you to forgive me and set me free from the curse of sin. I repent of these sins, and if there is still any darkness within me, I ask you to forgive me of that as well. I want nothing to keep me from the relationship with you that you desire for me. Please forgive me.

Father, you and I both know that I have said sorry so many times. But this time, I commit to walking away from these sins, never to return. My flesh is weak, but I commit to living by your Spirit, which gives me the power to never return to the sins I have confessed.

Thank you, Father, for your mercy. I don't deserve it, but I am so grateful. Thank you for forgiving me. In Jesus' name, Amen."

Renouncing

Now that you have confessed and repented, let's talk a moment to renounce those things in which you have participated. The word renounce means "to formally declare one's abandonment of a thing." You have confessed and repented and now it is time to formally declare that you are abandoning this lifestyle.

"Father, I renounce this lifestyle consumed with sexual immorality that I have lived. I formally declare in this moment that I abandon this lifestyle filled with lust and perversion and fornication. I renounce the things I've done that have led me away from the purity that you desire for me. I renounce the images I've seen, the videos I've watched, and the immoral actions I've taken. I renounce sexual addiction and choose your path, your plan, for my life. In Jesus' name, Amen."

Freedom

Finally, what you have been waiting for, FREEDOM! You should feel like a weight has been lifted from your chest. You should feel joy in your heart and a renewal in your spirit. And who the Son sets free is free indeed! Let's wrap this up by receiving your freedom and praising God for it!

"Father, by the power of the Blood of Jesus and the Holy Spirit, you have set me free! I receive that freedom now! No longer will I suffer under the yoke of slavery from sexual sin. I am free and I commit to staying free!

Father, I ask by your Holy Spirit that you give me every tool, every spiritual resource, everything I need to live a godly life. I commit my new life, my new freedom, to you, and choose from this moment on to walk in the freedom I was meant to have all this time. I choose purity. I choose holiness. I choose to be led by the Holy Spirit. Thank you for freeing me! In Jesus' name, Amen!"

Freedom. Doesn't it feel amazing! Praise God that you are free! I encourage you to call someone and share this news with them. Call a friend, a mentor, a pastor, a parent, a spouse, somebody and let them know that God has broken the chains of sexual immorality in your life. This is a great day! Celebrate it!

Now that you've calmed down a little from your celebration, it is time to use the tools you've learned to stay free. Christianity is not some easy walk in the park every day. Some days just might be, but Christianity is vigorous and requires your total attention. Make sure that nothing takes God's place as number one in your life. Renew your mind. Pray. Read the Word of God and let it live deep inside of you. Surround yourself with godly people at a truth-teaching, Spirit-led church. You can stay free if you use the tools God has provided for you!

I just want to say that I am proud of you. I spent many years a slave to sexual immorality but God is so faithful and merciful, and the feeling you are experiencing right now, I have experienced. You have taken a major step in your life. God has forgiven you and you are free, but God will also begin the process of restoring what has been lost. God will send what the Bible calls "times of refreshing" into your life (Acts 3:20). You may have thought before that your sin had disqualified you from the good things that God wanted to bless you with, and honestly, while you were deep in the muck, that may have been true. But now you are free and forgiven and you need to know that God is a God that delights in restoration.

I love what the Psalmist writes in Psalm 103:10-11.

> "He does not deal with us according to our sins, nor repay us according to our iniquities. For as high as the heavens are above the earth, so great is his steadfast love toward those who fear him"

Isn't that amazing? It is hard to believe he is that good to us, but he is! And he can restore! Allow God to restore what was lost. Lean on him. Trust in him. He is faithful.

I've told you a little of my story of sexual immorality and how it was a stronghold in my life, but let me tell you a little of how the story ends. Though I had fallen into sexual immorality in a variety of ways, once I walked through the process you just went through, God began restoring me. Shortly after that, I met the woman who would be my wife. I have often told her that when I look at her, I see God's grace. It's not just a nice thing to say to a pretty lady, but the truth. You see, I didn't deserve her. I had kissed other girls before, but I was her first kiss. I had failures with other girls before, but she was pure. And when I stood on that altar and committed myself to her, I didn't deserve the reward that she was and is today. But God is **so** good. He is so kind and gracious, and in that moment, I knew that he delighted in restoring his children.

He'll do the same for you, friend.

I pray God bless you and keep you. I pray you stay strong in the Lord and the power of his Holy Spirit. I pray God would protect you and keep you from evil. And I pray that when you encounter temptation, that the Holy Spirit will rise up in you, and no matter the attack, no matter the temptation, that you win, win win.

FINAL THOUGHTS
THE AFTERMATH

It is possible that you have read this book and have followed the instructions and still feel like there is something that is holding you back. Perhaps you have been so enslaved to sexual sin that you don't feel complete freedom, or at least like you thought you would feel.

Many times when dealing with setting people free, there are other factors that emerge in the process that reveal the enemy's plans, his attacks, his strongholds, his schemes, and these things have to be addressed in order to get complete freedom.

If that is the case, I don't want you to think your situation is hopeless, you simply need some personal attention as you walk this thing out.

I remember a time in my life as a teenager when I was having a rough time. I prayed about it. I asked God to help. I did those things I felt like I was supposed to do to get free from the situation. But it wasn't until I received some wisdom from the leaders around me that the root of the matter was revealed. God used them to dig deeper, and as we dug around, searching for what was left behind, God revealed a dark spot in my heart that I was able to recognize and address.

That may be your situation. If it is, I encourage you to do one of the following action steps. Before I list them, let me preface this by saying that these steps take into account that you are saved, you are filled with the Holy Spirit, you pray regularly, you read your Word daily, you are active in a local, truth-teaching, Spirit-led church, and you have at least one person serving as an accountability in your life. These are the Required Tools we discussed in earlier chapters, and if you remember, these things are necessary in order to beat this sin. So if you are in a place where you are not doing these things, I can say with a high percentage of probability that this is the problem. With that being said, If you are doing these things, and you still don't feel the freedom in your life like you expected, here are these additional steps.

1. **Talk to your accountability about how you are feeling.**
   Your accountability is there to see you through this situation. If you feel like you should be free at this point and are not, then discuss that and ask the Holy Spirit to reveal to one or both of you what the problem is.

2. **Get one on one guidance from a pastor, spiritual parent, or church leader.**
   If you need to follow through with some one on one advice, make sure it is someone in your life who has walked through the freedom process before so that you can get free.

   If you are unable to find help from one of these people listed, you may want to consider a professional therapist, however, it is *incredibly* important that if you do seek professional help, that you use a licensed, Christian professional. A Christian therapist will provide many of the same tools a non-Christian might, however, you will get the additional benefits of godly counsel, faith-building encouragement, and the addressing of spiritual issues a non-Christian might deem irrelevant.

3. **If you are a teen or are unmarried, speak to your parents. If you are married, speak to your spouse.**
   If you have been walking out this process but have been doing it secretly, hidden from people, especially a spouse, this could be the reason you haven't gotten totally free. I know there can be a fear of what will happen if certain people learn of your struggle, but, again, what is your freedom worth? Ask God to reveal to you how to proceed.

4. **Get a small team to regularly pray together.**
   The Bible tells us in Matthew 18:19-20,

   "I also tell you this: If two of you agree here on earth concerning anything you ask, my Father in heaven will do it for you. For where two or three gather together as my followers, I am there among them."

   If you are asking God to reveal what you've missed, it is a good idea to enlist a few friends and that you meet together at least weekly to pray together, in person, until the answer is revealed.

5. **Prayer and fasting.**
   It is possible that there is a spirit attached that doesn't leave so

easily. In Matthew 17, the disciples try to cast a demon from a boy and are unable. When they ask Jesus why, he responds,

"You don't have enough faith." And some manuscripts add in verse 21, " But this kind of demon won't leave except by prayer and fasting."

If you still feel enslaved, try spending some time praying and fasting to build your faith. When you fast, you choose an activity, like eating, television time, etc., and instead of doing that activity, you spend that time seeking God in prayer. I can say there are times in my life where praying and fasting have rally made the difference.

6. **You may be having spiritual muscle memory.**
    Muscle memory has been used to describe the observation that various muscle-related tasks seem to be easier to perform after previous practice, even if the task has not been performed for a while. It is as if the muscles "remember." In a spiritual sense, if you have been living a lifestyle that has been full of guilt from your failures, it could be that the enemy is still working to keep you feeling enslaved when God has set you free. I know it sounds weird, but if the enemy can't keep you enslaved, he will do everything he can to make you feel like you are.

    At this point it is important to rely on faith and genuinely believe what John 8:36 tells us,

    "So if the Son sets you free, you are truly free."

There could be a variety of reasons that could keep you from experiencing freedom, or from feeling that freedom. I encourage you, talk with someone about this. Don't keep it bottled in. One of the best tactics the enemy uses to keep us down is by convincing us that we can't tell anyone. Don't believe that! If you need further help, get it!

If you are connected to a quality local church, you are going to find people within who are committed to helping you get free. Take advantage of that! You wouldn't get sick and then refuse the help of a doctor. Don't do that with your church leaders either. They can help you walk you through this.

At New Covenant Church, we offer encouragement to people for a variety of issues. Whether they are financial, marital, struggles with addiction, sexual immorality, etc., the pastoral team is available to meet and encourage them, offer advice, and help them through the process. This may be your next step, whether it is at New Covenant or another quality church.

Wherever it may be, get that one on one help. You are going to overcome this! Have faith and believe that the good work God began in you will be completed.

Made in the USA
Columbia, SC
05 June 2024